MUHAMMAD ALI

MUHAMMAD ALI

A Biography

Anthony O. Edmonds

GREENWOOD BIOGRAPHIES

GREENWOOD PRESS
WESTPORT, CONNECTICUT · LONDON

WORCESTERSHIRE COUNTY COUNCIL		
335		
Bertrams	14.03.06	
796.83092	£16.99	
EVZ		

Library of Congress Cataloging-in-Publication Data

Edmonds, Anthony O.
Muhammad Ali : a biography / Anthony O. Edmonds.
p. cm. — (Greenwood biographies, ISSN 1540-4900)
Includes bibliographical references and index.
ISBN 0-313-33092-1
1. Ali, Muhammad, 1942– 2. Boxers (Sports)—United States—Biography. I. Title.
II. Series.
GV1132.A4E43 2006
796.83092—dc22   2005026171

British Library Cataloguing in Publication Data is available.

This book is included in the *African American Experience* database from Greenwood
Electronic Media. For more information, visit www.africanamericanexperience.com.

Library of Congress Catalog Card Number: 2005026171
ISBN 0–313–33092–1
ISSN: 1540–4900

First published in 2006

Greenwood Press, 88 Post Road West, Westport, CT 06881
An imprint of Greenwood Publishing Group, Inc.
www.greenwood.com

Printed in the United States of America

The paper used in this book complies with the
Permanent Paper Standard issued by the National
Information Standards Organization (Z39.48–1984).

10 9 8 7 6 5 4 3 2 1

To my wife Joanne and our three sons:
Anthony, Daniel, and Sam. For all your love and support.

CONTENTS

Photo essay follows page 62

SERIES FOREWORD

In response to high school and public library needs, Greenwood developed this distinguished series of full-length biographies specifically for student use. Prepared by field experts and professionals, these engaging biographies are tailored for high school students who need challenging yet accessible biographies. Ideal for secondary school assignments, the length, format and subject areas are designed to meet educators' requirements and students' interests.

Greenwood offers an extensive selection of biographies spanning all curriculum related subject areas including social studies, the sciences, literature and the arts, history and politics, as well as popular culture, covering public figures and famous personalities from all time periods and backgrounds, both historic and contemporary, who have made an impact on American and/or world culture. Greenwood biographies were chosen based on comprehensive feedback from librarians and educators. Consideration was given to both curriculum relevance and inherent interest. The result is an intriguing mix of the well known and the unexpected, the saints and sinners from long-ago history and contemporary pop culture. Readers will find a wide array of subject choices from fascinating crime figures like Al Capone to inspiring pioneers like Margaret Mead, from the greatest minds of our time like Stephen Hawking to the most amazing success stories of our day like J.K. Rowling.

While the emphasis is on fact, not glorification, the books are meant to be fun to read. Each volume provides in-depth information about the subject's life from birth through childhood, the teen years, and adulthood.

A thorough account relates family background and education, traces personal and professional influences, and explores struggles, accomplishments, and contributions. A timeline highlights the most significant life events against a historical perspective. Bibliographies supplement the reference value of each volume.

ACKNOWLEDGMENTS

Special thanks to the history department at Ball State University for providing me in 2004 and 2005 released time for my research, without which I'd still be writing the first draft of this book. I also appreciate the assistance of the coordinator of the department service center, Juneyetta Gates, and her capable student assistants, who helped in a number of ways. As always, the staff at Ball State's interlibrary loan service got me books quickly and didn't complain when I forgot to return them on time. Special thanks go to my student Hannah Weakley for helping me proofread the galleys in a most timely fashion.

I also want to thank three colleagues who labor in the field of sports history—Randy Roberts, Elliott Gorn, and Jeff Sammons—all of whom responded to my e-mail pleas for help in answering some difficult technical questions.

I would not have written this book had not Steven Vetrano, assistant editor in Greenwood's reference division, asked me to do so. I also thank him for his advice and his patience.

My greatest debt is to my wife of 41 years, Joanne Edmonds, and our three children, Anthony, Daniel, and Sam. They are, to quote a phrase, truly "The Greatest."

INTRODUCTION

The theme song from the popular television show *Cheers* concludes that the Boston bar that gave the series its name was an enticing home away from home because it was a place "where everybody knows your name." If that is the case, then, for Muhammad Ali, born Cassius Marcellus Clay, the world has been his *Cheers*. Probably no public personality since 1960—except for perhaps John F. Kennedy—has been more widely known and recognized throughout the world than this heavyweight prizefighter from Louisville, Kentucky.

Of course, millions of words have been spilled about Ali, from children's books that introduce him to young people to scholarly monographs that try to deconstruct his meaning. So why should there be yet another entry in the field of Ali studies? There is room for a brief biographical work that takes advantage of the most recent scholarship but is aimed at students, especially those in high school, who were barely even ripples on the gene pool when Cassius Clay won the heavyweight championship from Sonny Liston in 1964 and soon became Muhammad Ali. These students were in elementary school in 1996 when he carried the Olympic torch in Atlanta for its final few meters. Partly because this series is aimed at students, I will take more space discussing Ali's childhood, youth, and young adulthood than his career after 1975. Moreover, I will pay considerable attention to his actual bouts, especially the major ones, and less to his personal life, especially his various marriages. After all, Muhammad Ali was first and foremost an incredibly skilled prizefighter, and his success in the ring was the necessary condition for whatever larger role he played. Finally, this study examines that larger role and puts him a broader historical context that will help students understand that sport is always much more than what happens on the field or in the ring.

Although the heart of this book is the story of Ali's life and boxing career, I will also develop some larger themes about who he has been and what he has meant for the United States and the world. First, Ali fits into the classic American image of the so-called self-made man: his background was lower middle class, and he is an African American who confronted discrimination throughout his life. He rose from these conditions to the pinnacle of financial success and world recognition, largely through a combination of hard work and natural skills (and a lot of just plain luck). But he is also self-made in a more interesting psychological way. He has created many variations of himself. The mask metaphor works well here because Ali has literally created a series of personas that were often overlapping and sometimes contradictory. According to journalist Jack Newfield, Ali's various identities included "manchild, con man, entertainer, poet, draft dodger, rebel, evangelist, champion" (Hauser, 259). I would add to this list of personas: humanitarian, husband (often), father (many times), philanderer, patriot, Cassius Clay, and Muhammad Ali: The King of the World. I'll center my discussion around manchild, however, because for much of his life Ali alternated between being a kid and an adult.[1]

A second main theme grows out of the first. In many ways Ali has been more important for what he has represented than for what he is (and we may never know what that "is" is with this man of masks). Thus, much of what I present here will revolve not around Muhammad Ali as a person but rather as a cultural symbol, especially in the turbulent 1960s and early 1970s. His braggadocio, his religious conversion to the Nation of Islam, and his attitudes toward both race relations and hostility toward the Vietnam War in particular made him a hero not only to some Americans but also to many throughout the world. But probably even more Americans saw him as a pariah precisely because of these factors. Indeed, a major reason that I devote relatively little space to his life and career since 1975 is that after his victories over George Foreman in 1974 and Joe Frazier in 1975, Ali's major role in world history essentially dissolved almost into the realm of myth and legend. South Vietnam fell to the Communists in April 1975, thus ending the Vietnam War for all of its combatants and bringing an era to a close. Also by 1975, the civil rights movement had come to a virtual halt, having achieved almost all of its de jure goals, while by that year the black power movement of which the Nation of Islam was a part had virtually disappeared. In other words, the historical context that had helped propel Ali's importance beyond the ring had largely disappeared.

Interestingly, the past two decades have seen a growing sympathy, respect, and admiration for Ali, perhaps in part because he is no longer a cultural lightening rod and in many ways has become more calm. In spite of his debilitating struggle with Parkinson's syndrome, he has devoted considerable energy to raising money for the poor and pushing initiatives for world peace. Perhaps the epitome of his post-boxing career came when he carried the Olympic torch, that ancient symbol of amity and competition, on its final leg in the 1996 Atlanta Opening Ceremony. Now in his sixties, Muhammad Ali seems to have found a sense of inner peace, which may be his most lasting and real mask, or, more likely, not a mask at all.

NOTE

1. Perhaps there is something about boxing that brings out the kid in all of us, fighters and fans alike. Quite a few boxers adopted Kid as their nickname—Kid Chocolate, Kid Gavilan, Benny Kid Paret, Abe Kid Goodman, and Henry Kid Matthews among them. Maybe they hoped that this linguistic marker of youth would somehow intimidate their opponents. Muhammad Ali had others means to do this.

TIMELINE: SIGNIFICANT EVENTS IN MUHAMMAD ALI'S LIFE

1942	Born Cassius Marcellus Clay Jr., on January 17
1954	Bike stolen; begins training to be a prizefighter
1954	First Golden Gloves Championship
1959	First hears of Elijah Muhammad, head of the Nation of Islam (NOI)
1960	Registers for the Vietnam War draft
	Wins Olympic gold medal in light-heavyweight division
	Throws medal into the Ohio River after a racial incident in Louisville
	Angelo Dundee becomes trainer
	Wins first professional fight against Tunney Hunsaker
1961	Wins eight bouts, six by knockouts
	Becomes more involved with the NOI
1962	Wins six bouts, the most important one over former light-heavyweight champion Archie Moore
1963	Wins three fights, two by knockouts
1964	Stunning upset of Sonny Liston to win heavyweight championship
	Announces his conversion to the NOI
	Elijah Muhammad gives Cassius his Muslim name, Muhammad Ali
	Classified 1-Y (not qualified to serve) by his local draft board after failing to meet minimum standards on mental ability test
	Marries non-Muslim Sonji Roi

1965	Defends title against Liston, winning with a first round knockout
	Defends title against former champion Floyd Patterson
1966	Divorces Sonji
	Successfully defends title six times, with five knockouts
	Declared 1-A (fit to serve) by local draft board after minimum standards lowered by military
	Makes infamous "I ain't got no quarrel with them Viet Cong" comment
1967	Successfully defends title twice
	Marries Belinda Boyd, an NOI member
	Refuses induction into the Army; boxing license revoked by state boxing commissions
	Stripped of heavyweight championship
	Found guilty of violating Selective Service Act; sentenced to five years in prison and fined $10,000. Appeals conviction.
1967–70	Banned from boxing
1970	Fights Jerry Quarry after state of Georgia sanctions bout; wins by knockout
1971	License restored in New York in court decision
	Loses to Joe Frazier in 15 rounds
	Supreme Court reverses conviction for violation of Selective Service Act
	Wins North American Boxing Federation (NABF) championship against Jimmy Ellis
1972	Successfully defends NABF title four times
1973	Loses, then regains NABF title against Ken Norton
1974	Defeats Joe Frazier in 15 rounds, retains NABF title
	Upsets champion George Foreman in Zaire, Africa, winning World Boxing Association (WBA) as well as World Boxing Council (WBC) titles, retains NABF title
1975	Successfully defends championship titles four times, most notably defeating Joe Frazier in a 14th round TKO in the "Thrilla' in Manilla"
1976	Successfully defends title four times, most notably defeating Ken Norton in a 15 round decision
1977	Successfully defends title twice
	Divorces Belinda, marries Veronica Porsche, not an NOI member

1978	Loses championship to Leon Spinks in a 15 round decision
	Regains championship from Spinks in a 15 round decision
1979	Announces retirement
1980	Comes out of retirement, loses to champion Larry Holmes
1981	Loses to Trevor Berbick
	Officially and finally retires
1984	Diagnosed with Parkinson's Syndrome
1986	Divorces Veronica, marries long-time friend Lonnie Williams, not an NOI member
1990	Informally visits Iraq, prior to the Gulf War and helps convince Saddam Hussein to release some hostages
1996	Carries the Olympic Torch on its final leg of the Opening Ceremony, lights Olympic Flame in Atlanta
2002	Watches daughter Laila win her first boxing title
2003–present	Living in Michigan with his wife, Lonnie, awaiting the opening of the new headquarters of the Muhammad Ali Center for the Advancement of Humanity, scheduled for November 2005 in Louisville

Chapter 1

BOXING IN ITS HISTORICAL AND CULTURAL CONTEXT

Muhammad Ali's career is only a slender thread in the fabric of boxing history, and boxing is only a minor part of the general topic of sport. So if we want to understand why Ali became an authentic world hero to many and villain to others, we need to put him into historical context. It is especially important to see him in relation to sports in general, boxing in particular, and especially to two previous black heavyweight champions, Jack Johnson and Joe Louis.

Sports have only recently been studied by serious historians. They have realized that because so many people engage in or watch sporting activity, it would be folly for scholars to ignore the role of athletics in modern life. As sports historians Randy Roberts and James Olson rightly point out, for Americans "sport [has] become a national obsession, a new cultural currency, a kind of social cement binding a diverse society together." Indeed, they argue, "Instead of work, family, or religion, increasingly large numbers of Americans have been choosing sport as the focus of their lives" (Roberts and Olson xii). In other words, sports bring people and communities together around a common interest and passion; successful teams provide a kind of civic pride unavailable from other venues.

Americans' fascination with sports no doubt derives from a variety of other sources as well. Paradoxically, in addition to serving as that social cement, sports can also provide a connection to a more individualist past. In some ways, sporting events can be linked to the United States' mythical frontier days, when men faced numerous obstacles, both natural and human, and overcame them through skill and pluck. Although clearly cooperation was necessary, our mythical heroes are individuals such as Daniel Boone and Davy Crockett. As historian Roderick Nash puts it: "Whether clearing the forests or clearing the bases, . . . victory was the result of superior ability. The sports arena like the frontier was pregnant with opportunity for the individual. The start was equal and the best man won. Merit was rewarded" (Nash 127).

Students of sports have also noted the way in which successful athletes serve as heroes and role models for sports fans. From Babe Ruth, Red Grange, and Bill Tilden in the 1920s to Michael Jordan and Billy Jean King in the later twentieth century, individual athletes have provided vicarious, even cathartic thrills to millions of their fans. To sociologist Janet Harris, such sports heroes helped "define individual and collective identity, compensate for qualities perceived to be missing in individuals or society, display ideal behaviors, . . . and provide avenues for temporary escape from the rigors of daily life" (quoted in Riess 309).

The concept of sport as character-builder strongly complements this individualistic tendency. Obviously, few would argue that merely watching an athletic event somehow turns the spectator into a better person. Participation in sports, however, can become the crucible in which strength of character is molded. Sportswriter John Tunis waxes eloquent on the value of competitive sports: "The joy of struggle is an element of growth that, once experienced, a youngster never forgets" (Tunis 6). That joy, then, can lead to a sense of determination to see it replicated. Sports also provide lessons in public and civic virtue. Young Americans who are active in sports have to learn to sacrifice themselves for the common good and to obey the rules and decisions of those in authority even when those decisions seem unfair. Tunis offers us a rhetorical question: "may it not be that a basketball game won or lost is worth a hundred lessons in civics in the classroom?" (Tunis 6). His answer is clearly a resounding "Yes!" The stadium, court, and ring become a microcosm of what is best in the American democratic value system. One learns to play by the rules, to accept adversity or triumph, to locate the middle way between individual effort and pulling together as a team, and perhaps most important, to be a good sport.

Finally, many argue that sports are crucial as an avenue for social mobility. A major portion of U.S. mythology is taken up by the image of rags to riches. Frontier experience emphasized the triumph of individualism and saw a place for the rise from poverty to plenty through this individual effort. Andrew Carnegie could indeed congratulate young men born poor because according to him to be born "to that ancient and honor able degree . . . renders it necessary that they should devote themselves to hard work" (quoted in Edmonds 16). Of course, we should not necessarily pat a poverty-stricken lad on the back, urging him to count that destitution as his greatest blessing. For some, athletics in the twentieth century has provided a way out of unfortunate circumstances. How else, except through sports, could a man like Babe Ruth with such a humble and unsavory background gain such hero status except through sports? In addition, sports historians such as John Tunis have argued that participation in sports has provided a vehicle for assimilation in American society as well, helping thousands of immigrants reach the goal of "complete acceptance and complete Americanization" (Edmonds 17).[1]

Clearly, sport looms large in the life of many Americans—and indeed the global community—and deserves careful study. That said, those who write seriously about boxing and boxers face the uncomfortable fact that of all the major sports in the United States, prizefighting probably has the most questionable reputation. Yet the sport obviously has its defenders, from boxers and managers to sportswriters attracted to the glitter of the ring to a handful of academic historians. And if sports in general have been seen to have a useful, purgative role in modern life—providing a sublimated and safe working out of competitive instincts—certainly boxing, which ideally pits two people in direct physical conflict, should provide the most immediate form of catharsis.

Boxing may well be the most natural of all athletic contests. Sportswriter John V. Grumbach contends, "Were mankind to follow the laws of nature, the fist is to man what horns are to the bull, claws and teeth to the lion and tiger." Indeed, Grumbach goes on to suggest that a "wiser human race might well forbid any other weapon of combat and be better off" (Edmonds 17).

Boxing's proponents admit that the sport is a relatively harsh one. Historian Alexander Johnson says, "Fighting with fists, whether 'the raw uns' or gloves, is not a gentle sport.... Blood will always be shed, eyes will be blackened, and there may be accidents of a more serious nature" (Edmonds 17). However, although hardly gentle, boxing is not necessarily brutal. If both fighters are well-trained and conditioned with relatively equal skill levels, they suffer little lasting pain. Even a knockout, according to Johnson, "which looks brutal, is not much harder to take than chloroform" (Johnson 10).

Indeed, to some observers the harshness and physical preparation required by prizefighting make the sport a symbol of a nation's masculinity. Writing in the eighteenth century, Pierce Egan, one of the first students of boxing, suggested that those who excoriate boxing no doubt

"prefer effeminacy to hardihood-assumed refinement to rough nature."
These naysayers are people "whom a shower of rain can terrify, under the
alarm of their polite frames, suffering from the unruly elements" (Edmonds
18). Presumably, then, the death of boxing would presage the withering
away of the nation itself.

Closely related to the portrait of boxing as symbol of national manli-
ness is the connection between boxing and individualism. Unlike football, boxing is not a team sport. To be sure, the prizefighter is surrounded
by a cluster of camp followers: manager, trainer, owner, sparring partners,
and the rest. But the actual contest pits lone person against lone person.
The victory, at least in the eyes of the public, belongs to the individual
who proved best. According to Nash, boxing heroes abounded in the
1920s, that transitional decade between an older frontier United States
and a confusing, frightening urban nation. It is no accident that boxing's
first million-dollar gates came in this decade when millions of Americans
sought for their solace surrogate frontiersmen. Nash points out that wor-
ship of individual heroes, such as Jack Dempsey and Gene Tunney, out-
stripped admiration for sports teams. To Nash, the popularity of boxing
indicated a great deal about the American character: "In a nation not
oblivious to the approach of middle age, it was comforting to count the
heavyweight champion of the world among the citizenry. Here was evidence, many reasoned, that the nation remained strong, young and fit to
survive in a Darwinian universe" (Edmonds 18). And survival, of course,
is a function of the time-honored American value of individual initia-
tive.

According to its chroniclers, the sport of boxing has a long, if not
honorable history. The sport goes back at least 3,500 years to ancient
Crete, based on evidence uncovered in archeological excavations. We
know that some form of prizefighting existed in both Greece and Rome,
but from the fall of the Roman Empire to the early eighteenth century,
no records of boxing exist. Boxing apparently was reintroduced in
England around 1700, and by 1719 a man named James Figg had battered
enough opponents to be generally considered the champion of the
nation.

For the next one hundred years, Englishmen dominated boxing. There
is general agreement that prizefighting as a distinguishable sport in the
United States arrived around 1800, beginning among slaves in the South
and spreading gradually northward. The United States' first recognized
fighting champion was an ex-slave, Tom Molineaux, who fought the
English champion, Tom Cribb, in 1810. Throughout much of the nineteenth century, however, boxing remained a relatively minor sport, gen-

erally associated with the lower classes. One of the reasons for this lack of popularity, no doubt, involved the legal difficulties boxers could encounter. As late as 1889, not a single state legally permitted prizefighting. Fighters ran the risk of getting thrown in jail and paying heavy fines for taking part in the outlawed sport. Moreover, early boxing was a physically dangerous endeavor. There was no medical supervision, no doctors appointed by boxing commissions, in fact, no boxing commissions at all. Serious injuries were common.

It was not until the advent of John L. Sullivan, "the Boston Strongman," in the late nineteenth century that prizefighting in the United States developed an authentic hero and became a major sport. Prior to Sullivan's emergence, boxing retained an unsavory reputation. Many observers saw it as sport closely identified with both the lower classes and immigrants, who fell into the hands of crooked promoters who rigged fights and bilked both the boxers and fans who gambled on the outcome. According to boxing historian Nat Fleischer, when Sullivan stepped down as champion, "prize fighting was beginning to be regarded as a clean sport, boxers were beginning to be men of higher caliber, promoters were beginning to be businessmen instead of swindlers, and followers of boxing were well on their way to being substantial, decent people" (Fleischer xi).

Sullivan's monumental impact on prizefighting was, in part, technical. Because he was a rushing, punching fighter, he was handicapped by traditional bare-knuckle rules, which allowed both wrestling and stalling tactics. Because he was a public hero, he could successfully demand, and popularize, the so-called cleaner glove fighting, thus eliminating from most of his bouts much of the opportunity for dirty fighting and crookedness. The technical changes in prizefighting congruent with Sullivan's career pale before the legend this man created.

Of course, he was a powerful, skillful fighter. But more, Sullivan was a symbol of toughness and virility to a generation of American males. His bouts drew huge crowds, and his exploits were reported in the nation's major newspapers as he became a personification of national glory and the pride of young American males. Sullivan's essential masculinity also revealed itself outside the ring. He was a public orator who compared himself to politician Roscoe Conkling; using his fame as a fighter, he went on the stage, and his reviews and pageants garnered public acclaim. He was even loved despite his personal exploits. He was a joyous public drunkard and, although married, lived openly with a burlesque dancer. Yet even in the late Victorian Age, no one seemed to mind very much. Imagining John L. Sullivan dead and in heaven, Nat Fleischer contends that not a laugh would be heard "when the big fellow with the handlebar mustache signals for a cup of mead, and rumbles, 'My name is John L. Sullivan, and I can lick any son of a bitch in the place'" (Fleischer xiii). When Sullivan finally lost his championship to James Corbett in 1892, few of Sullivan's fans could really admit that their hero had fallen even though Corbett had, in fact, beaten an overweight middle-aged man.

Sullivan was responsible for one additional alteration to prizefighting: in effect, he established the color line in boxing. There were a number of superb black heavyweights fighting in the 1880s and 1890s, most notably, Peter Jackson from Australia. Yet Sullivan refused to fight any black boxer. In the 1880s he claimed that his hesitancy was financial, fearing that black fighters would not meet his price. But by 1892 he maintained simply, "I will not fight a Negro. I never have and never shall" (Edmonds 21).

Black fighters, then, were effectively barred from heavyweight championship bouts throughout the rest of Sullivan's ascendancy. But in the first decade of the twentieth century, a black boxer emerged whose prowess was impossible to ignore. After a string of nonchampionship victories, Jack Johnson, the black challenger, finally caught up with champion Tommy Burns in Sydney, Australia, put up the requisite purse, and proceeded to pound Burns senseless. On December 26, 1908, Johnson became the first black heavyweight champion of the world.

It is crucial to describe Johnson's image as champion because both Joe Louis, the second black champion, and Muhammad Ali, the subject of this biography, consistently found themselves linked to Johnson, although in very different ways. There is little doubt that, at least among whites in the United States, Johnson was the fight game's most unpopular champion. Few denied the man's ability in the ring. Renowned sportswriter Grantland Rice summed up expert opinion when he noted, "Johnson had the fastest pair of hands I've ever seen in a big man. Nobody has come close to him as a defensive master and counter puncher" (Edmonds 21).

Superb fighter that he was, Johnson functioned with several handicaps. He became champion at a time when legal segregation and virulent racism were reaching an apogee in American life. Most Southern states had imposed rigid legal segregation of blacks in all public facilities—from schools to transportation to entertainment venues. The state of South Carolina went so far as to mandate separate Bibles for blacks and whites testifying in court cases. And ex-Confederate states managed to virtually eliminate black voting through ploys such as a tax on voting and literacy tests graded by white voting registrars. Finally, and most terrifying, thousands of black Americans were lynched in the late nineteenth and early twentieth centuries.[2]

Thus, the mere idea of a black champion severely challenged certain white assumptions, particularly when that black man became champion by beating a white man. Attitudes at the time suggested that a prizefight between white and black boxers might well resemble or even lead to a racial war. Furthermore, Johnson's antics in the ring did nothing to soothe the white fear of a black champion. "Papa Jack," as he was known, was a great taunter and joker in the ring. Flashing a monstrous smile, highlighted by his golden front tooth, Johnson seemed to enjoy pummeling his white opponents. This tactic became especially newsworthy in 1911 when Johnson went up against former champion Jim Jeffries. Defenders of white supremacy cajoled the 35-year-old Jeffries, retired for six years, to become the "Great White Hope" and "shut Johnson's smiling mouth once and for all" (Roberts 89). Jim Jeffries no doubt felt the weight of the whole white world on his shoulders. Johnson slaughtered the aging giant. What galled many whites the most was that beginning in the third round, Johnson began to tease the ex-champion and chat with the spectators. Such bad form and unpredictability caused considerable nervousness in the white community. It is not surprising that racial disturbances broke out all over the country after Johnson's victory, leaving a number of people dead and wounded. These riots would typically begin when outraged whites picked fights with African Americans who were peacefully celebrating Johnson's victory. Such affray helped convince the white boxing establishment to work toward resegregating the ring in the future.

Had Johnson been merely an uppity black man in the ring, perhaps his image would have been less negative. Outside the ring, however, he violated the most sacred of racial canons: he consorted with white women and even married one while he was champion. According to most students of Johnson's career, these women were probably no better than prostitutes. But the white community fiercely resented his seeking out these women and flaunting them in public. Ultimately, Johnson's assignations with white women got him into trouble with the law. In 1910 Congress passed the Mann Act, making illegal the transporting of women across state lines for immoral purposes. In 1913, Johnson was convicted (probably unfairly) of violating that act, and to avoid prison he fled the country. He did not fight another major bout until 1915 when Jess Willard, the latest White Hope, knocked him out in Havana, Cuba.

Johnson's fellows in the boxing fraternity, no less than the public, passionately disliked the black champion. In fact, Tommy Burns, whom

Johnson defeated for the crown, claimed that Johnson's color caused him to lose the fight because his hatred of the black man distracted him. The disgust with which the populace looked on Johnson is summed up in the thunderous welcome Jess Willard received in 1915 after defeating Johnson. Three thousand people met his train at Pennsylvania Station in New York City, even though it arrived at night. After being cheered by mobs who lined the streets, he embarked on a two week stint at a local theater recreating his victory (at $5,000 per week). Willard then embarked on a successful vaudeville road tour, sparring a bit and even displaying his skill as a horseman. His glory confirmed on the basis of one questionable knockout, Jess Willard was cheered as the man who ended the shameful reign of Jack Johnson.[3]

The history of boxing between Johnson's defeat and the emergence of Joe Louis need detain us only briefly. Students of the sport generally agree that the 1920s was a golden age of prizefighting. Dominated by the rugged puncher, Jack Dempsey, and his conqueror, Gene Tunney, boxing achieved both respectability and wide popularity. Perhaps no other fight in boxing history up to that point drew such attention as the second Dempsey-Tunney bout in September 1927. More than 100,000 people saw the battle and paid a record $1,658,660 to watch Tunney win. Indeed, as boxing chronicler John Durant notes, this fight was in many ways the climax of that golden age of sports.

Between the retirement of Tunney in 1928 and the rise of Joe Louis in 1935, boxing entered its so-called dark ages. Between 1930 and 1935, the heavyweight championship changed hands five times, and none of the titleholders were particularly glamorous or competent. The last of the five, James Braddock, who won the championship in 1935, refused to defend it for two years. It seemed as though boxing, similar to the nation's sagging economy, was dying. It was generally agreed among members of the boxing fraternity that a new hero—a great fighter and appealing human being—was needed.

Certainly few believed that such a champion would be anyone but a white man. Yet in 1934 when he turned pro, a young black man from Detroit, Joe Louis, emerged as the most exciting and proficient heavyweight in the world. He won the championship from Braddock in 1937 and successfully defended it an astonishing 25 times during the next twelve years. But had it not been for the creation of a carefully orchestrated public persona as the polar opposite of Jack Johnson, Louis would probably have never been given a chance to fight for the title. Louis's managers, black businessmen John Roxborough and Julian Black, created a list of rules for Louis that must never be violated, including:

He was never to have his picture taken with a white woman.

He was never to gloat over a fallen opponent.

He was to live and fight clean (Young 16).

Louis followed this "not Jack Johnson" formula for most of his professional career. With the exception of some rabidly segregationist Southern newspapers, most white observers praised Louis for being a "good Negro." Adjectives such as "modest," "unassuming," and "clean-living" dotted white journalists' reports on the "Brown Bomber," as Louis came to be known. White observers often specifically contrasted Louis's demeanor with Johnson's. According to sportswriter Richard Vidmer, "Comparing Joe Louis to Jack Johnson is like comparing Lou Gehrig [a squeaky clean New York Yankee baseball star] to Al Capone [the infamous gangster]" (Edmonds 65). For Nat Fleischer, Louis's greatest accomplishment lay in the fact that during his 12-year reign as champion, there was little agitation for him to be "dethroned by a white man" (Edmonds 66). A letter of advice to Louis from a white minister in late 1935 epitomized the attitudes of most whites toward the up and coming heavyweight:

Some day I feel that you will be the champion, and should this come to pass, try always to be the champion of your people, so that when you are no longer the champion, the world will say of you—he was a black man outside, but a white man inside, most of all in his heart (van Every 74)

As patronizing and racist as such a letter seems today, it represents the view of most whites in this time period, a view that Louis and his handlers felt obliged to take into account for purely pragmatic reasons: "no more Jack Johnsons" was the operating mantra of the white-controlled boxing world.

Louis's image in the black community was more complex. While some African American observers praised him because he was respected by whites and had achieved a certain level of mobility that might inspire black youth, most maintained that his great accomplishment was strengthening racial self-respect. Dozens of African-Americans recall his victories with a fierce pride. Malcolm X remembered that after the Braddock fight "all the Negroes in Lansing...went wildly happy with the greatest celebration of race pride our generation has ever known" (Edmonds 98). So powerful a symbol was Louis that a black man on death row in Mississippi in the late 1930s cried out as cyanide gas entered the chamber, "Save me Joe Louis, save me Joe Louis, save me Joe Louis" (King 111).

Louis's rise to fame was, however, marred by one unexpected defeat. In 1936, he suffered a twelfth-round knockout at the hands of German Max Schmeling, which stunned the boxing world. Similar to mythological fallen heroes, however, Louis was able to rise from the ashes of defeat to vault even higher in public recognition and adulation. His ability to be all things to all people culminated when he defeated Schmeling in a 1938 rematch in slightly more than two minutes of the first round. Whites and blacks alike celebrated the victory as Louis avenged his only professional defeat up to that time. Most Americans saw the victory as a symbolic triumph over Nazi militarism and racism. One unidentified correspondent crowed that "the bright, shining, shimmering symbol of race glory has been thumped into the dust" (Edmonds 80), while in Biloxi, Mississippi, a white matron and her black maid hugged in a fervor of American patriotism (personal recollection of the author's mother). Even four years after the bout, Louis's victory resonated when an American general introduced Louis to a crowd of soldiers as "the first American to K.O. a Nazi" (Edmonds 84).

Louis confirmed this image of Americanism when he joined the Army in 1942 even though he was exempt from the draft. Turning down a commission, he enlisted as a private and spent his tour of duty putting on boxing exhibitions for other American servicemen. About his decision, he said simply, "I am very anxious to go overseas and help get this war over with. I'm glad I'm an American citizen" (Louis 163). Interestingly, he also used his time in the military to quietly work toward lessening the impact of racial segregation in the Army, openly opposing regulations that forced blacks to sit in the back of busses in the South. But such modest protests received little publicity.

Between 1949, when Louis officially retired, and 1960, boxing experienced a checkered history. When Louis attempted a comeback in 1950 (for financial reasons), he defeated eight nobodies before being humiliated by young white powerhouse Rocky Marciano in 1951. Although the 1950s witnessed a boom in televised boxing that was watched by millions, television saturation caused a decrease in the popularity of local boxing clubs. By the late 1950s, audiences began to wane. Moreover, in the early-mid-1950s, boxing at all levels was penetrated by the influence of organized crime figures such as Bernie Carbo, who controlled several fighters and their television appearances and caused a number of bouts to be thrown.

Certainly, when Marciano won the heavyweight championship in 1952, he brought a high level of interest and integrity to the sport. But when he retired in 1956, an unexciting black fighter named Floyd

Patterson took the crown, lost it briefly in 1959, and regained it in 1960. Although perceived as a decent person in the Joe Louis mold, Patterson was, according to most observers of boxing, dull and pedestrian. Prizefighting doldrums, however, were about to receive a shot in the arm. Cassius Marcellus Clay Jr., a brash young black heavyweight from Louisville, Kentucky, who called himself "the Louisville Lip," won the Olympic light heavyweight championship in the summer of 1960 and turned professional that fall. Boxing would soon have a new heavyweight champion whose remarkable career would make him both a national hero and villain. He would become a figure of international renown who both revivified his sport and transcended it.

NOTES

1. Certainly, athletic prowess does not guarantee social mobility or assimilation. Most high school athletes, for example, never play on collegiate teams, much less reach the professional ranks. The same is true for most immigrants. Yet because of the attention focused on a few super stars, especially since the post–World War II growth of television, the myth of mobility through sports has maintained a strong hold on many Americans, especially African Americans including, as we shall see, Cassius Clay. For a discussion of this issue, see Harry Edwards, *The Revolt of the Black Athlete* (New York: Free Press, 1970); and Jack Olsen, *The Black Athlete: A Shameful Story* (New York: Time-Life Books, 1968).

2. In one Kentucky town, spectators could pay a dollar admission and bring their guns to the local Opera House. They then fired from front row seats at a black man who had been captured by a mob of angry whites and bound on the stage.

3. Johnson claimed that he had thrown the fight in order to get his Mann Act sentence reduced to a fine, but there is no corroborating evidence to support this assertion.

Chapter 2

THE LIP IS LAUNCHED: CASSIUS CLAY EMERGES, 1942–1960

I am the greatest.
    —Cassius Clay, on countless occasions during his career

Cassius Marcellus Clay Jr. was born on January 17, 1942, in Louisville, Kentucky, tipping the scales at his first weigh-in at a less than impressive 6 pounds, 7 ounces. His only sibling, brother Rudolph, was born two years later. For those who fancy astrology, Cassius was born under the sign of Capricorn, the Goat—the sign that supposedly produces the most stable and serious people in the zodiac. According to astrology, Capricorns are "calm, unemotional, and cautious to the extreme" ("Capricorn"). These are hardly the qualities that have come to be associated with Cassius Clay. Perhaps the Chinese zodiac offers a more accurate picture; Cassius was born in the Year of the Horse, and horses are described as "very independent, cunning people" who need "to guard against being egotistical" ("Chinese Zodiac"). Among projected careers for people born in that year is poet. Close, but there is no record that anyone associated with the youngster even believed an ounce of astrology. What his family did believe, although perhaps in retrospect, was that Cassius was an extraordinary baby.

His mother, Odessa Grady Clay, traced her lineage back as far as her paternal grandfather, an Irishman named Abe Grady. Indeed, she kept a picture of her father prominently displayed on her mantle piece, proudly noting that he appeared to be white. And she also boasted that her son was partly white, a heritage that did not please Cassius later in life. As he once told a racially mixed audience, "My white blood came from slavemasters, from raping. When we were darker, we were stronger" (Olsen 56). Actually, Odessa's lineage was based on marriage, not rape. Abe Grady migrated from Ireland to the United States and married a black woman; a son from this marriage also married a black woman, and they became the parents of Dessay Grady Clay.

Cassius's father, Cassius Sr., claimed to be a descendent of Henry Clay, the great American Whig Party politician and presidential candidate. While this assertion smacks a bit of family legend, more probable is the family story that Cassius Jr.'s paternal great-grandfather had been a slave freed by Cassius Marcellus Clay, a famed nineteenth-century Kentucky abolitionist, whose name our young Cassius bore. In fact, Odessa convinced her husband to use the name. This original Clay was a character of mammoth physical and moral proportions. At six feet six inches tall, he was a commanding presence as he led troops in the Mexican-American War. When he returned from that conflict, he became one of the first white Kentuckians to free all his slaves, much to the ire of his fellow citizens. He dismissed death threats and contested the slavery issue throughout his home state. During one such debate, he was stabbed in the chest and probably survived only because he was able to stab his opponent back. This Clay kept his trusty Bowie knife at the ready. His saga lasted well into the post–Civil War period. When he was 84 in 1894, he employed his even trustier cannon to drive off a posse who believed that he had kidnapped a 15 year old girl; actually, he had married her! As with his Brady ancestors, however, when Cassius became a Muslim, he rejected what he termed his "slave name," something of an irony given the original Clay's passionate hatred of slavery and very interesting life (Remnick 82).

Cassius's parents can best be described a members of the Southern black middle class. Although hardly wealthy, especially by white standards, the Clays were certainly better off than the families who brought us some of Cassius's most notable opponents, especially heavyweight champions Floyd Patterson, who grew up one of eleven children, and Sonny Liston, whose father had 25 mouths to feed.[1] Cassius Sr. was a sign painter and part-time artist who worked hard to earn a living, while his mother sometimes cooked and cleaned for wealthy white families. The Clays could afford to pay $4,500 for a house. Although a small cottage in an all-black area, it was far from the poorer all-black district known as Smoketown. As journalist David Remnick suggests, "The Clays never wanted for the basics of life" (Remnick 82). So in at least a fundamental economic sense, Cassius was sheltered from the hardships of life in ways that many other black children growing up in the 1940s and 1950s were not. He never had to take a job to help support his family (although he did clean blackboards and desks at Louisville's Spaulding College to earn spending money); he had a pet chicken and dog; and even owned an electric train set. Significantly, as we shall see later, he also sported a brand new red and white Schwinn bicycle, which cost $60 at the time (the equivalent of $411 in 2003).

His mother, Odessa, stoutly maintained that young Cassius experienced an almost idyllic babyhood and childhood. She wrote a biography of her son, carefully scripted in ink on notebook paper, and delighted in telling her son stories about his babyhood. She remembered that he was always an active energetic baby who learned to walk at 10 months, ran everywhere rather than walking, and danced on his toes as a small child. Indeed, an enduring theme in Odessa's hymn of praise to her son is that the child was father to the man. Looking back, she saw all sorts of prefigurations of future greatness. Not only did he dance on his toes, according to his mother, but he also delivered a mean punch. She said that when he was six months old, he stretched his arms and "hit me in the mouth and it loosened my front tooth and affected my other front tooth so I had to have both of 'em pulled out." She concluded, almost joyously that "his first knockout punch was in my mouth" (Olsen 65). His strength appeared in other ways as well. He spent a lot of time standing up in his baby bed, shaking it furiously. On one occasion, he cried out "Gee, Gee," which Cassius later claimed stood for "Golden Gloves"—a championship he later won (Olsen 65).[2] Whenever Odessa took her young son out for a walk, onlookers were convinced, they told her, that she had given birth to another Joe Louis. His mother claimed that her son was basically fearless, as well. The only thing that really frightened him as a child was a fur piece similar to one worn as a coat collar. She used it to convince him to obey her. In addition, he was simply beautiful. Cassius recalls his mother often telling the tale of his birth: "She said that I was such a pretty baby, everyone thought I was a girl" (Ali, *Butterfly* 4).

Young Cassius also had quite a gift for gab, according to his parents. "He just loved to talk," Odessa remembered. "He tried to talk so hard when he was a baby. And people would laugh and he'd shake his head and jabber fast[er]" (Olsen 65). According to his father, when Cassius was eight, he loved to gather little neighborhood boys around him and yack at them through to bedtime. Again, in retrospect, his family saw the man's qualities in the child.

Yet we know from Cassius himself, as well as other sources, that his childhood was not entirely a bed of roses. To be sure he never starved, but he suffered in a number of ways. Indeed, he told sportswriter Jack Olsen that his first memory was of his mother telling him that because he'd eaten a green apple, he might come down with a fatal disease (Olsen 67). He also recalls being afraid of several neighborhood children and participating, usually with some reluctance, in the inevitable rock fights that the little boys got into.

There was a deeper fear, however, one that Cassius did not talk about a great deal: domestic violence in his family. Cassius Sr. was profoundly frustrated professionally. Although he made an adequate living as a sign painter, he wanted to be a "real" artist, painting murals and canvases. According to David Remnick, however, his work was "garish" and "a step above kitsch." Nonetheless, Cassius Sr.'s self-perceived failure grated on him (Remnick 85). No doubt this was a contributing factor to his battles with alcohol. As British author John Cottrell coyly put it, the senior Clay developed "a taste for gin" (Cottrell 11).

Even without the impact of alcohol, Cassius Sr. was "a cock of the walk, a braggart, a charmer, a man full of fantastical tales and hundred proof blather" (Remnick 84). His father may well have been the main influence that led to Cassius Jr.'s penchant for cockiness. His talk was essentially harmless unless he had too much to drink; then he could become violent. Louisville police arrested him six times, including twice for disorderly conduct. His wife called the police several times to report physical abuse by her husband. Usually, he was put under a security bond until he sobered up. On at least two occasions, one in the Clay home, Cassius Sr. was apparently stuck with a knife. In addition, he was a ladies' man who would cruise bars at night to pick up women. At one point after her son's rise to fame, Odessa got so fed up with such behavior that she filed for a separation.[3]

Although Cassius and his younger brother, Rudolph, always claimed that their childhoods had been "happy and peaceful," the two boys "grew up in an atmosphere of impending explosion" (Olsen 71). We can only speculate about the impact of his father's unpredictability (and Cassius's tendency to deny the problem) on the youngster. It might well have been a major factor in his burning desire to make something of himself.

The atmosphere of racial tension in post–World War II Louisville no doubt also contributed to Cassius's development in his formative years. His father was a major influence on his racial views. Cassius Sr. bitterly blamed white racism for forcing him to quit school in the ninth grade and for closing off the possibility of becoming a true artist. He admired black nationalist Marcus Garvey's call for race pride and self-sufficiency and his castigation of white people. The elder Clay seemed to have an inherent distrust of whites.

Young Cassius absorbed his father's teachings. He recalls, for example, that as a 10 year old he "would lie in bed at night crying as he wondered why the black people had to suffer" (Cottrell 12). Personal experience only served to confirm his father's views of whites. Cassius remembers well his mother's story of an early "encounter with prejudice." While the two were waiting at a bus stop on a hot day, Odessa asked a white employee at a diner if she could have a cup of water for her thirsty son. "The man said he could not help us and shut the door in our faces." Most painful was Cassius's attempt to "imagine the pain my mother felt when she tried to find the words to explain" the incident (Ali, *Butterfly* 10). He also chafed when whites cut in front of him in line and felt ashamed when his mother trudged across town to do the dirty work for white people. He was especially upset that all the pictures of Jesus and the angels he saw were of white people. He recalls asking his mother if blacks were even allowed in heaven. When she said, "Naturally," he decided that all the black angels must have missed the photo shoot because they "would be in the kitchen preparing the milk and honey" (Ali, *Butterfly* 13).

But perhaps the defining moment in his racial education came when his father told him about the murder of Emmett Till. Till was a fourteen year old Chicagoan who was brutally murdered in August 1954 while visiting relatives in Mississippi. He had allegedly said "Bye, baby" to a white clerk, whose husband and half brother, offended at this breach of race etiquette, had pistol whipped, shot, and dumped the young man into the Tallahatchie River. An all-white jury acquitted the two clearly guilty men in 67 minutes. Said one juror, "If we hadn't stopped to drink pop, it wouldn't have taken that long (Remnick 88). The elder Clay made sure that his boys looked at the photographs of Till's horribly mutilated face to learn the lesson of white justice.

The Till incident and other experiences of racial slights fed into the young Cassius's growing desire to escape the kind of discrimination that limited economic opportunity and stung the soul. After Cassius became a professional fighter, he claimed that he started boxing because it was the fastest way for a young black man to achieve social and economic mobility. Because he knew he wasn't very bright, he figured he couldn't go to college and become a football or basketball star. But prizefighting was different: "A boxer can just go into a gym," Cassius said, "jump around, turn professional, win a fight, get a break, and he's in the ring" (Remnick 88). And when he had achieved a little success, he craved material status symbols: a huge mansion, big cars driven by chauffeurs, and bodyguards.[4] For him, Hell would be "earning twenty-five dollars a week, with four hungry children crying at home because they were hungry" (Cottrell 13). Cassius also might have developed an interest in boxing because of an incident when he was a small child. He remembers that Cassius Sr. once took him to a particular tree in Louisville and told him to look at it carefully, even to touch it lovingly. When young Cassius asked why, his father said simply, "Joe Louis leaned against that tree." Cassius remembers shivering and thinking, "What would it be like to be a fighter as great as Joe Louis?" (McRae 329–30).

Of course, Cassius's rise would not be that simple, but it was remarkably rapid. His lifelong commitment to boxing began because of a theft. When he was 12, he realized a major youthful ambition. He became the proud owner of a bicycle—not just any two wheeler, but a top of the line red Schwinn. He was so proud of his new status symbol that he spent the first day he owned it showing his prize around the neighborhood. On the next day, he and a friend rode downtown to a merchants' exhibition, which was giving away popcorn and ice cream. After a few hours of free food that was no doubt bad for them, the young Cassius discovered that his bike had been stolen. In tears, he ran to the basement of the nearby Columbia Gym, where he had been told a policeman was often around. Angry, screaming for a statewide manhunt, and threatening to "whup" whoever stole it, Cassius met the man who would be the first great influence on his boxing career (Cottrell 15). Joe Martin was a white Louisville policeman, but his real passion was prizefighting. He had been an amateur boxer in college at the University of Arizona and spent most of his spare time training youngsters to fight in the Golden Gloves. Martin detected something special in the young man's passion and advised him to take a few boxing lessons before he tried to "whup" anyone.[5]

Initially, Cassius didn't take up Martin's offer, but two weeks later the young Cassius was mightily impressed when he saw Martin and some of his fighters on a Louisville television show called "Tomorrow's Champions," which featured local bouts. Cassius was intrigued by the idea that if he boxed, his friends would see him on television. As early as 12, then, he seemed to have a substantial ego and sense of the power of the tube. So he dragged his brother Rudolph to the Columbia Gym and presented himself to Martin.

Cassius Clay was no easy trainee, however. He was so loud and full of himself that Martin actually occasionally banned him from the gym. Moreover, Cassius was not very well liked by other young boxers who were in Martin's stable, mainly because he was such an obnoxious self-promoter. As Martin recalled, "He was always bragging that he was the best fighter in the gym and that someday he was going to be champion" (Torres 80). Moreover, Martin at least initially thought that Cassius had no more potential than many of the other kids he helped. But the youngster came along well enough—especially under the tutelage of Martin's black assistant, Fred Stoner—and after six weeks Martin thought he was ready for his first fight.

As Cassius had hoped, his initial bout did appear on "Tomorrow's Champions," as he took on a young white boxer named Ronnie O'Keefe (who, similar to Cassius, weighed in at 89 pounds). Cassius admits that he was frightened as he walked toward the ring with his father and saw that O'Keefe was older and looked more experienced. Cassius Sr. said, significantly, "We're going to whup him" (Ali, *Butterfly* 19). In three two-minute rounds, the boys mainly flailed away at each other with huge 14-ounce gloves, until each youngster had a headache. Cassius apparently struck flesh slightly more often than Ronnie because he won a split decision. He certainly saw the barely achieved victory as a profound omen, however, as he yelled into the ringside camera that he was on the way to becoming "the greatest of all time" (Remnick 92). He might also have trumpeted the possibility that he would also become the most lippy, ostentatious champion of all time, or at least since Jack Johnson.

That first bout did not impress Martin very much. His young fighter still "didn't know a left hook from a kick in the ass," the crusty policeman asserted (Remnick 92). Part of the problem may have involved a street fighting bully named Corky Baker, who terrorized his school and neighborhood with stunts such as dangling football players over balconies and beating up on smaller kids like Clay. Cassius dared him to enter the ring, and when Baker accepted (after being shamed into it by taunts from his buddies), Cassius beat him soundly. Before the end of the 2nd round, Cassius recalls, "he said 'This ain't fair' and ran out of the ring" (Ali, *Butterfly* 24). This was an enormous boost to Cassius's already sizeable ego, and he got much better. He combined fast hands and feet with extraordinary reflexes and a powerful work ethic. He labored tirelessly in the gym, skipping rope and shadow boxing. Most mornings, he would even challenge his school bus to a foot race. Much like the young Joe Louis, he didn't smoke or drink or do drugs (except for a few times when he and his friends would sniff gas fumes, an exotic exercise he soon left behind him). He also became a fanatic about what he saw as nutrition: he carried around garlic in a bottle of water to combat high blood pressure and claimed that soft drinks were in the same health-destroying league as cigarettes.

During the next two years, he fought a number of amateur fights, averaging about one every three weeks and winning consistently. He would come home after a victory and tell his parents what he screamed after that first fight—that he was destined to be champion and that he would buy them a house and cars, the stuff of the American dream. In 1956, he continued to shine as he made his first appearance on the local sports page and won his first Golden Gloves championship, in the Novice Division. Although the diagnosis of a heart murmur (which proved to be inaccurate) kept him out of the ring for four months in 1957, by the end of that year he had won more fights and developed considerable confidence. In fact, when the up and coming light heavyweight Willie Pastrano was in Louisville for a fight, Cassius found out, called Pastrano, and asked if he could come to his hotel room to talk, proclaiming to be a great fighter who would win the gold medal in the 1960 Olympics. As Pastrano's manager, Angelo Dundee, recalls, a curious Pastrano said, "What the Hell. There's nothing on TV" (Remnick 97). Cassius asked question after question about training techniques and strategy, showing remarkable determination for a 15 year old. When Pastrano was in town later for another fight, a 17-year-old Cassius asked to spar with him. Pastrano agreed and was pounded by the faster, younger Cassius. Pastrano didn't like the fact that an unknown amateur made him look bad but admitted to Dundee, who tried to make excuses for his fighter, that Cassius had "beat the Hell out of" him (Remnick 98). Ironically, Angelo Dundee would become Cassius's trainer from the time he turned pro until the end of his career.

Cassius continued to win most of his fights, although he did lose to an older boxer named Green when he was 16. He was also knocked cold by one of his sparring partners but came back the next day utterly unfazed. But his life outside the ring was less successful. Although quite handsome and a bit of a flirt, Cassius had little confidence around girls. Areatha Swint, one of his high school classmates, recalls dating him for a while. The young Cassius seldom complimented her. Instead, "he was more interested in [heavyweight champion] Floyd Patterson." After three weeks of courting, he finally asked if he could kiss her: "I had to teach him. When I did, he fainted" (Remnick 94).

Cassius's life in the high school classroom was equally problematic. He entered Central High School, Louisville's largest black high school, when he was 15 and struggled to master academic challenges. His grades as a sophomore were so abysmal that he had to withdraw for the next year. But when he returned, he managed to impress Principal Atwood Wilson, especially with his fierce dedication to training. (He woke at 5:00 A.M. almost every morning and did his roadwork in heavy shoes in a local park). Wilson decided to encourage Cassius, as he took a page from Cassius's book and boasted in school assemblies that the young man would be heavyweight champion of the world someday. Ignoring complaints by many teachers, Wilson did not keep Cassius from graduating in spite of his failing to meet the school's requirements. The proud principal maintained that "in one night he will make more money than [I] and all you teachers make in a year" (Remnick 95). And he wanted to claim such a future example of fame and fortune as a Central High product. He stated baldly that Cassius would pass even if every teacher failed him. Wilson won that bout, but in something of a compromise, Cassius Clay graduated in June 1960, finishing with a class rank of 376 out of 391, but only with a certificate of attendance, not a diploma. (Cassius would always have trouble reading; members of his entourage would often have to read his multitude of press clippings to him.)

Obviously, boxing would be Cassius Clay's life. By the time he graduated, he had won a hundred bouts, while losing only eight. Among his major victories were two national Golden Gloves titles in 1959 and 1960 and two national Amateur Athletic Union light heavyweight championships, also in 1959 and 1960. Also in those two years, events occurred that would loom large later in his career: in 1959 in Chicago, he first heard of Elijah Muhammad and the Nation of Islam (NOI); and in April 1960 the 18-year-old Cassius registered for the military draft.[6] He also continued to hone his persona. A born showman, he concluded early in his career that mere boxing excellence would not draw huge crowds and earn great kudos. He had to have a shtick. He started reciting poems, for example, predicting the round in which his opponent would fall: "This guy must be done/I'll stop him in one."[7] He also recognized, as he put it, that "fight fans acted like kids from my school days" (Torres 86). Because they wanted to be entertained, Cassius was willing to mouth off and promote himself to anyone who would listen. At one amateur tournament Cassius actually distributed glossy pictures of himself. Even as an amateur he wanted to provoke people with his braggadocio; then, because of his reputation, people would come to his fights hoping that someone would close his increasingly famous Louisville lips. He had also developed a trademark style, in which he taunted opponents in the ring and challenged them by dancing around, often with his arms at his side, daring his rival to swing. This style would be very controversial among boxing's old guard. Sarge Johnson, who coached the 1976 U.S. Olympic boxing team, for example, told his fighters, "I don't want you to watch Ali [Clay]. He does too many things wrong" (Cassidy 23). With his remarkable combination of skill and personality, Cassius was ready for the world stage. Indeed, he even dreamed of turning pro immediately after high school, but Joe Martin convinced him to slow down. His career would receive an instant boost should he win an Olympic medal. "The Olympic champion is as good as the number ten ranked pro," Martin told Cassius (Cottrell 25). And the young Clay accepted the advice. He would make the initial steps toward his first entrance on that world stage at the United States Olympic Trials in San Francisco in May 1960.

NOTES

1. When Liston noted this fact at a Senate hearing into mob influence on boxing in the 1950s, Senator Everett Dirksen (R-Ill.) observed that Sonny's father was "a champion in his own right" (Remnick 48).

2. The Golden Gloves bouts are part of regional and national amateur boxing tournaments held annually since 1923. They have usually been sponsored by local newspapers and divided into several weight and experience divisions. Most boxing observers perceive a Golden Gloves championship as an important sign of skill and a possible future in the professional ranks.

3. To this day, Ali defends his father. He dedicates his most recent memoir, *The Soul of a Butterfly,* to his mother and father. In it, he does admit that Cassius Sr. "at times had a quick temper" but nonetheless was a loving man who especially enjoyed kissing his oldest son (Ali, *Butterfly* 4).

4. Joe Louis was not immune to the lure of big cars. After the defeating Primo Carnera, he told his good friend Jesse Owens that he intended to buy "the snazziest car in Detroit" (McRae 97).

5. Looking back on his childhood, Ali thinks that at least one aspect of his boxing skill manifested itself even earlier. He recalls that as a small child, he would have his brother Rudy throw rocks at him, Rudy, but could never succeed in hitting him: "I was too fast," Ali remembers. "I was running left, and right, ducking, dodging, and jumping out of the way" (Ali, *Butterfly* 5–6). A premonition of the Ali shuffle, perhaps.

6. For the sake of stylistic variety, I will sometimes refer to the NOI as "the Black Muslims," the name the white press generally gave the group.

7. Cassius's pugilistic idol Joe Louis also predicted the round in which he would knock out Primo Carnera, the opponent in his first major bout. He did so more modestly, however, saying "that he would do his best to knock out Carnera within five rounds" (McRae 37). He missed by one round; Primo went down in the sixth.

Chapter 3

THE LIP ARRIVES:
MAY 1960–JUNE 1963

Because he won a national Amateur Athletic Union (AAU) title in 1960, Cassius Clay earned a spot at the Olympic boxing trials in San Francisco. Getting there was something of an adventure, however, because Cassius was deathly afraid of flying. When his flight encountered a thunderstorm over Indiana, Cassius prayed with such fervor that he apparently almost drowned out the sound of the engines. When he arrived safe but still shaken, he was by far the most publicized of the prospective Olympians, in part because word of his outspoken personality had preceded him. He was also the most experienced competitor in the light heavyweight division, if not the whole competition. He did receive some bad press because of his reputation as a braggart, however, so much so that Martin extracted a promise from Cassius to keep his lip buttoned. Even so, he was roundly booed during his second elimination fight. At a sleek 175 pounds and superbly conditioned, Cassius, most observers assumed, was a shoo-in to win the Olympic bid if not the hearts and minds of fight fans. But his opponent in the championship bout on May 20 was no pushover. Alan Hudson, representing the U.S. Army, was a tough, experienced boxer. During the 1st round, he launched a left hook that Cassius never saw. Landing on his head, it sent him to the canvas. After an even 2nd round, Cassius went to work. In the third he caught Hudson square on the jaw coming out of a clinch, then pummeled the young soldier so savagely that the referee stopped the fight. As a footnote to the experience in San Francisco, Cassius—perhaps recalling the turbulence of his previous flight—was so frightened about flying home that after the Olympic trials, he threw away his return airline ticket to

Louisville, borrowed money from a referee, and took a train back to Kentucky.

Later that summer, Cassius went to New York City where a young reporter named Dick Schapp interviewed him as he showed him and another fighter around Harlem. They saw a black nationalist—perhaps a member of the Nation of Islam, more commonly known to whites as "Black Muslims"—preaching on a street corner about the need for self-sufficiency. Cassius must have recognized the approach because it mirrored the economic black nationalism pushed by his father. The group stopped at a restaurant owned by the famed middleweight champion Sugar Ray Robinson, one of Cassius's idols. When Robinson arrived in a purple Cadillac, his worshiper was so in awe that he didn't seem to notice that Robinson barely noticed him, mumbling a brief "Hello" and walking regally into his establishment. Cassius exclaimed to Schapp, "Someday I'm going to own two Cadillacs—and a Ford for just getting around in" (Remnick 101). Interestingly, looking back on the event, Cassius realized that he had been deeply hurt by Robinson's cavalier attitude: "At that moment, I vowed never to turn a fan away." He also had a long memory. The final time he saw Robinson, not long before the great middleweight died in 1989, Cassius said, "I [am] still waiting for that autograph!" (Ali, *Butterfly* 32, 37).

Also during his stay in New York City, Cassius breezed into the office of Madison Square Garden official Teddy Brenner and said without pausing, "My name is Cassius Clay. I'm going to the Olympics, I'm gonna win a gold medal; I'm gonna be the next heavyweight champion of the world; and I want to borrow ten dollars" (Hauser 42). The stunned Brenner gave him the ten spot and filed his name away for future notice, especially when Cassius actually paid back the money after the Olympics.

After this interlude, Cassius faced the daunting prospect of flying to Rome for the Olympic Games. It was a minor miracle that the new U.S. Olympic light heavyweight champion ever made it to Europe, given his fear of flying. He informed Martin that there was no way he'd risk his pretty face on an international flight. When it proved impossible to book a berth on a ship, Cassius concluded that Rome would survive without him. Martin jawboned his protégé for two hours before he convinced Cassius that if he did not fight in the Olympics, his professional boxing career was more likely to crash and burn than an aircraft crossing the Atlantic. So Cassius Clay went to the 1960 Olympic Games.[1]

Cassius had a blast in Rome. Almost from the moment of his arrival, he was the talk of the Olympic Village. He hit the ground boasting, telling everyone who would listen and many who wouldn't that he was going to win the championship in his division. His great exuberance and engaging naiveté generally trumped his cockiness. He eagerly participated in the Olympic tradition of exchanging national badges and buttons. As one teammate put it, "Cassius made a career of it," weighed down by as many as 43 of them. "He was like a kid in fairyland" (Olsen 83). He also dashed around chatting up competitors from other countries. He was so popular, according to another teammate, that if the Village had held a mayoral election, Clay would have won it. American track sensation Wilma Rudolph, who won three gold medals herself, said that Cassius's "peers loved him. Everybody wanted to see him. Everybody wanted to be near him" (Remnick 102).

Of course, the main reason Cassius was in Rome was not to garner badges and buttons but to win a medal. He easily dispatched his first opponent, Yvon Becaus from Belgium, with a technical knockout in the 2nd round. In his quarter final bout against a former gold medalist, Soviet Gehadiy Schatkov, Cassius won a clear decision after blackening both of his adversary's eyes. His opponent in the semifinals, Australian champion Tony Madigan (whom Cassius had decisioned in 1959), actually thought he had won the three-round fight; the judges disagreed, awarding Cassius the decision.

Cassius faced a more stern test in the finals on September 5, 1960. His opponent, Zbigniew ("Call me Ziggy") Pietrzykowski, was a skilled Polish fighter who had won the bronze medal in 1956. Nine years older than Cassius with more than 230 fights to his credit, Ziggy was also a southpaw, and lefties had usually been troublesome for Cassius. The Pole had special incentive because in the bout immediately preceding the light heavyweight championship one, an American middleweight, Sergeant Cook, had won an unpopular decision over a fellow-countryman. In the 1st round, Ziggy looked appropriately fired up as he punished the Louisville youngster pretty badly. By the end of the 2nd round, Cassius had abandoned his show-offy style and landed some solid straight blows. But, as he indicated after the fight, "I knew that I had to take the third round big to win" (Cottrell 29). And he did just that, using his quickness and a series of combination punches that left the Pole reeling. At the end of the fight, Ziggy was slumped on the ropes, almost knocked cold. The five judges voted unanimously that Cassius Clay was the Olympic Light Heavyweight Champion. According to Martin Kane in *Sports Illustrated*, Cassius's championship was "the most popular" of the three American boxing victories. Kane worried that Cassius had "never caught a hard punch," however, and speculated whether he could "take it if hurt." Cassius's response—no doubt part of his showman/exaggerator mask—was simply, "Man, I don't want *ever* to get hurt" (Kane 31).

The young man was obviously overjoyed. He carried his Gold Medal with PUGILATO ("Pugilist" in Italian) emblazoned on it wherever he went. According to Wilma Rudolph, "No one else cherished it the way he did." He even wore it to bed, noting that he had to sleep on his back for the first time or else "the medal would have cut into my chest" (Remnick 103). What ultimately won that medal, according to Jack Olsen, was simply conditioning: "He worked like a coolie, from the age of twelve on, to sharpen himself into the best fighting machine of his era" (Olsen 87).

But there were some interesting grumblings. Many senior sports writers came of age when Joes Louis and Rocky Marciano set the standard for how the best fighters would fight—standing up, boring in, flattening the opponent. These writers complained that Cassius's style in most of the rounds he fought violated these almost sacred pugilistic traditions. Long-time boxing writer A. J. Liebling thought that Cassius lacked the "menace" to be a truly great big man. His "skittering style" just didn't scare enough people, and if he danced too much when he fought longer bouts, he seriously risked "deceleration" (Remnick 103). One wonders if Cassius had this advice in mind when he created the rope-a-dope strategy against George Foreman 14 years later.

Cassius also took some verbal shots from anti-American communist bloc reporters. When a Soviet journalist pestered the champ about how badly blacks were treated in the United States, Cassius responded that in spite of problems, the United States was still "the best country in the world, counting yours."[2] Shortly after he returned to Louisville, he published his first poem, reflecting his pride as. an American. He bragged about winning Gold for the United States:

So I beat the Russian and I beat the Pole
And for the USA won the Medal of Gold (Marqusee 48).

He was also badgered about whether and when he would turn pro. He replied simply, "I want money, plenty of it, and it looks like I got a talent for boxing. Why not make the most of it?" (Cottrell 310). Later he told an interviewer that he would rather become a pop singer like Elvis Presley; fortunately, this was only a passing fancy.

Significantly, shortly before he left Rome, Cassius saw people gathering around professional Heavyweight Champion Floyd Patterson, who had come to watch the Olympic bouts. Cassius admired Patterson, to the extent of writing a poem of praise when Patterson regained the heavyweight crown from Sweden's Ingemar Johansson. Determined to meet him, Cassius introduced himself and was greeted by "a milquetoast hand-shake" of congratulations. As with Sugar Ray Robinson earlier that summer, Cassius felt slighted, perhaps expecting Patterson to join the crowd of adulators: "It hurt me," Cassius admitted. "That cat insulted me and someday he'll have to pay for it" (Remnick 104). A prophetic remark indeed, and one that stayed with Cassius.

When Cassius arrived in New York on his way to Louisville, he stayed for a while. He and reporter friend Dick Schapp, who had met him at the airport, went to a shop that made fake headlines and had one printed up that said, simply, "CASSIUS SIGNS FOR PATTERSON FIGHT" (Remnick 104). While in the Big Apple, Cassius ate what he thought was an excessively pricey meal, $2.50, at Jack Dempsey's restaurant; had his first taste of alcohol—a drop of liquor in a Coke; and stayed in a suite in the posh Waldorf-Astoria Hotel. The accommodations were paid for by William Reynolds, a wealthy Louisville magnate who hoped to woo Clay into letting him develop a plan for the young boxer's professional career. He also gave Cassius enough money to buy watches for his parents and brother at Tiffany's. When an exhausted Schapp pleaded to call it a night, Cassius insisted that the two of them adjourn to the champ's room where they poured over the young boxer's ever expanding scrap book.

When he returned to Louisville, Cassius received a hero's welcome. Mayor Bruce Hoblitzell, along with cheerleaders and hundreds of fans, were waiting on the tarmac at Standiford Field Airport. A triumphant motorcade wound up at Central High School, where more cheerleaders and a huge banner, trumpeting "Welcome Home Champ" awaited the school's most famous "graduate." The mayor addressed a crowd of more than a thousand fans, proudly asserting that "if all young people could handle themselves as well as [Cassius Clay] does, we wouldn't have any juvenile problems" (Olsen 86). The mayor was especially impressed by the modesty with which Cassius carried his honors. When Cassius arrived at his house on Grand Street, he found that Cassius Sr. had painted the front steps red, white, and blue; father greeted son with a rendition of "God Bless America," an odd choice for a man who so thoroughly distrusted the whites who dominated the United States.

Cassius continued the celebration for a few more weeks. At one point, when Wilma Rudolph came for a visit, he stood up in the back of a pink Cadillac, shouting, "I am Cassius Clay. I am the greatest," as he and Wilma tooled down the streets of Louisville. He also proclaimed Ms. Rudolph "the greatest," clearly forgetting what he learned about the uniqueness of superlatives in high school (Remnick 106).

Although seemingly ecstatic over the fame and acclaim Cassius brought their city, some of Louisville's movers and shakers had profoundly ambiguous feelings about the champion's race. For example, even though the local Chamber of Commerce had given Cassius a nice citation, it refused to host a dinner for him, claiming that it just didn't have any spare time to prepare such a fete. Later when one of Cassius's financial backers took him for a meal at the all-white Pendennis Club, he received a stern letter of reprimand. Race inevitably bubbled under the surface. And one wonders if the mayor had revised his view of Cassius's ability to set an example for young people.[3]

If Cassius noticed such subtle slights, he didn't mention them at the time. He was having too much fun as he continued to sport that medal. Indeed, constant use was beginning to wear off some of the gold. Ultimately, however, pleasure had to give way to business if he were to turn his fame as an Olympic Champion into the kind of career he envisioned. Initially, a number of boxing folks were sniffing around. Former Olympic Heavyweight Champion Pete Rademacher made inquiries, and Archie Moore gave Cassius a business card. According to boxer and Cassius biographer, Jose Torres, manager Cus D'Amato tried to use Torres as "an intermediary" to get to Clay (Torres 96). At one point Cassius had hoped that Ray Robinson would consent to train him, but he was not interested. In his most recent memoir Cassius says that he offered Joe Louis the position of manager but that the Brown Bomber turned him down because "Joe was the quiet type, and he didn't like loudmouth, bragging fighters" (Ali, *Butteryfly* 36). It was Billy Reynolds who made the first firm offer, which included a salary for Clay no matter how his fights turned out, and a trust fund. The deal also included a provision that Joe Martin would continue to manage the young professional. To Reynolds's dismay, the Clay family rejected the offer, ostensibly because Martin had no experience managing professional fighters. In fact, according to David Remnick, Cassius Sr. "saw Martin as the embodiment of...the white Louisville police who had arrested him more than once" (Remnick 107).

The elder Clays found the next offer—with Martin out of the picture—much more to their liking. When Reynolds refused to desert Martin, Louisville businessman William Faversham put together a syndicate of some of the wealthiest men in the state to back Clay in his professional career. Each of the 11 partners contributed $2,800 to the kitty. Clay received a $10,000 lump sum for signing the contract, minimum guaranteed earnings of $4,800 in each of the initial two years of the deal, and the right to draw out up to $6,000 until the contract expired in 1966.

Clay and the syndicate would split gross earnings down the middle, while the group paid for training and travel expenses. Finally, 15 percent of any money Clay made would be put into a pension fund; however, Cassius would have preferred that it go into real estate. He complained that he wanted to be able to "point at a lot with an apartment on it and say 'That's mine.'" Showing his lack of comprehension of financial matters, he worried that the bank where his pension money was kept "might burn down or something" (Remnick 110). But given the propensity of prize-fighters in the past to squander their earnings, the syndicate was no doubt wise to enforce this provision.

Who were these 11 paragons of the local business community, and why would they want to get involved in the somewhat disreputable sport of boxing? After all, the stench of Bernie Carbo and mob involvement in boxing still hung over the sport, especially around an up and coming heavyweight named Sonny Liston. Faversham was a vice-president of Brown-Foreman Distillers, producers of the popular Early Times and Old Forester bourbons; Patrick Calhoun was a retired businessman and horse breeder; William Cutchins headed Brown-Williamson Tobacco; Vernter Smith was a successful salesman, formerly at Brown-Foreman; William Brown was chairman of the same company; Archibald Foster headed the local branch of a New York advertising firm that handled the Brown-Williamson account; Elbert Sutton had large holdings in U.S. Steel; George Norton IV was an officer of the local television station that broadcast *Tomorrow's Champions*; fellow media mogul Robert Bingham owned the two major Louisville newspapers as well as the CBS affiliate; J.D. Coleman owned businesses in Florida, Georgia, Illinois, and Oklahoma; and finally, the youngest of the group (at age 26) was James Ross Todd, scion of a famed Kentucky family, who said frankly that he made his money by "wheeling and dealing" (Remnick 108).

Interestingly, except perhaps for media men Norton and Bingham, none of the investors appeared to have much interest in or knowledge of prizefighting. Calhoun admitted almost total ignorance, while Brown's only connection to Clay was that his aunt cooked for one of Brown's double first cousins. Perhaps part of the motive was civic pride; after all Cassius's Olympic victory brought a good deal of national attention to Louisville. Owning a piece of a potentially famous fighter would bring a bit of social caché as well; Clay would be a useful bauble to talk about, enlivening dull board meetings.

On the other side of the coin, perhaps this local power elite, fearing that Clay's ever-growing mouth might bring shame to the city, wanted to be able to rein him in if necessary. As one member of the syndicate put it, the official line was that Louisville's movers and shakers wanted "to improve the breed of boxing, to do something nice for a deserving, well-behaved Louisville boy, and finally to save him from the jackals of boxing." He added, however, unofficially, that he would also like "to make a bundle of money" (Remnick 109).

Whatever the motives of its members, the Louisville Sponsoring Group, as the syndicate called itself, used its financial support to free Cassius Clay to work on his prizefighting skills. He made his professional debut on October 29, 1960, taking on Tunney Hunsaker, who in his spare time was the police chief of Fayetteville, West Virginia. The Louisville promoter Bill King chose Freedom Hall as the venue and advertised the bout as the first pro fight for the Olympic champion. Some 6,000 enthusiastic fans showed up, which provided plenty of money for King to meet his $2,000 guarantee to Cassius. Clay claimed that his opponent was "a bum" and that he would "lick him easy" (Cottrell 47). But he must have been a bit concerned because he prepared thoroughly under the tutelage of local trainer Fred Stoner, rising most mornings at 5:00 A.M. for a two-mile run before sparring with his brother, Rudolph. Hunsaker actually recalls seeing Clay in a sporting goods store the afternoon of the fight, looking distinctly nervous. Cassius's first opponent, with 17 professional victories and only 8 defeats, obviously was more experienced than the Louisville youngster, and Cassius could not put him on the canvas in the six-round bout. Nonetheless, the grossly overweight Hunsaker was clearly beaten, as Clay's nimble footwork and barrage of left jabs compensated for his lack of a knock-out punch. He won easily if not spectacularly. Hunsaker was gracious in defeat. He told a friend after the fight that Clay would someday be heavyweight champion and concluded that "it was an honor for me to have been in the ring with him" (Hauser 31).

Faversham, convinced that his fighter needed some high powered outside assistance, enrolled him in Archie Moore's California training camp soon after the Hunsaker fight. Moore had fashioned a remarkable career. He won his first bout in 1935, knocking out Piano Man Jones in the 2nd round; he was victorious in his final bout in 1963, dropping Mike DiBrase in the 4th round. During this 27-year span, he knocked out 141 opponents, more than anyone in the history of boxing, and for a time was lightweight champion. His longevity suggested a fine boxing intelligence. In addition, Moore, similar to Clay, was a man of masks. While Cassius affected the braggadocio of the playground combined with his father's fast mouth, Moore came on like a fancy music hall Britisher. Clay and his owners hoped that the old dog could teach the young pup some of his ring savvy.

In some ways, Moore's facility was quite foreboding. He called it the Salt Mine, with the gymnasium bearing the colorful nickname, the Bucket of Blood. In the sparse grounds outside the gym, Moore had arranged several boulders, each inscribed with the name of a famed former boxing superstar—Jack Johnson, Joe Louis, Ray Robinson—as if the ghosts of the past were sternly watching the champions of the future. Moore was initially impressed with Clay's work ethic. As in Louisville, he was up early for his morning runs, tackling the steep hills that surrounded the camp. Moore didn't object to Cassius's unusual boxing techniques, with dropped hands and intricate footwork. Indeed, he thought his style combined with his speed would stand him in good stead: "In the back of my mind, I thought to myself, here is someone who could have knocked out Joe Louis" (Remnick 112).

But the youngster and the veteran, in spite of their age differences, both had massive egos that often clashed. Clay chafed at advice he didn't like, as when Moore advised him on how to achieve early knockouts. Clay proudly indicated that he wanted to fight like Sugar Ray Robinson, still his idol, not Archie Moore. He was even more upset by the camp's Spartan regimen, which required its participants to wash dishes and keep the camp clean. Clay, whose mother had spoiled him where household tasks were concerned, balked, convinced that he was no dishwasher. He did the chores reluctantly and made it clear to Moore that he was unhappy. Moore remembers that he wanted Clay to respect him but that the young heavyweight was often contentious. Clay even challenged Moore to a sparring match, to which the reigning light heavyweight champion frostily responded, "I don't box with amateurs" (Hauser 33). Ultimately, Moore called Faversham to complain; the two decided that Cassius was less than mature and probably needed a good spanking. Barring that eventuality, Cassius simply returned to Louisville.

While the Moore experiment was going sour, the syndicate was in search of an appropriate trainer. Lester Malitz, who had once produced television fights for the clients of syndicate member Archie Foster, and Harry Markson, the president of Madison Square Garden Boxing in New York, recommended Angelo Dundee (who had previously met Cassius while in Louisville with one of his charges, Willie Pastrano). One of Dundee's brothers (among seven children of illiterate Italian immigrants) was a prizefighter, and another brother, Chris, became a manager. After serving in the Navy, Angelo joined Chris in 1948, and they established a boxing camp in Miami Beach in the early 1950s. A far cry from Archie Moore's spacious outdoor venue, the Dundees ran their operation out of the 5th Street Gym—in the vivid words of David Remnick, "a rat-infested, termite-ridden walk-up," which could be accessed only through an unmarked door. A staircase about to collapse led the visitor to the second floor and a classic boxing character who guarded the entrance. Emmett "the Great" Sullivan, with his raggedy clothes and unlit cigar, demanded a 50 cent admission fee (Remnick 114). In this forbidding environment, Dundee trained successful fighters such as Pastrano, Luis Rodriguez, and Sugar Ramos. He was also known as one of the best in the business at repairing cuts and staunching bleeding when his fighters were getting pummeled.

Aware of Dundee's solid reputation, Faversham journeyed to Miami Beach in the winter of 1960 to offer him a job as Clay's trainer. Dundee recalled that his meetings with Clay in Louisville had shown that Cassius was a bit of a nut but nonetheless profoundly committed to learning all he could about boxing. Cassius Clay was a quick study. Dundee agreed to become Clay's trainer for $125 per week in addition to bonuses.

Cassius showed up in Miami before Christmas even though Dundee had wanted him to spend the holiday at home. Dundee put him up at a hotel that was a notorious hangout for various unseemly sorts including pimps, prostitutes, gamblers, and drunks. Clay was not tempted by the pleasures of the flesh and bottle. Indeed, the local lowlifes became attached to the young fighter and would take him to nightclubs to hear the latest in black music. While they got soused, Cassius sipped orange juice and left for home early. He did, however, have one complaint about his accommodations. His roommate, a young Caribbean fighter whom Dundee picked out to keep Clay company, had apparently never heard of deodorant: "He was a clean kid, but he stunk," Cassius observed (Torres 101).

Ever the early riser, Clay would start each day of training at 5:00 A.M. with roadwork. As he ran from his hotel to the gym, police would sometimes get complaints that a young black man was running down the street. In a southern city during the era of segregation, such a black male must obviously have been guilty of something. The police, who were aware that Dundee had a new black fighter under his wing, always called to make sure Clay was the runner. In other words, Angelo Dundee took care of his charge.

More than that, Dundee genuinely liked and respected Cassius and certainly knew how to handle him. He wasn't bossy like Moore, and as Dundee put it, he didn't train Clay, he "directed him," in part because Cassius was a self-starter. Dundee said he was "like jet propulsion. Just touch him and he took off" (Hauser 36). He also did not try to reign in Clay's lip, recognizing that it was a pose that would quite clearly fill arenas with paying customers. He brought his charge along slowly and even though Cassius bragged mightily about wanting to fight heavyweight Floyd Patterson as soon as possible, Dundee matched him only against opponents who would challenge but not overmatch him.

Clay was happy to work with Dundee. He told biographer Jose Torres that Angelo never tried to hector him or tell him "when to run, [or] how much to box. I do what I want to do." Assuming his bantering mask, he also told Torres that he was convinced that Dundee was "half-colored" and that he was only passing as an Italian. He concluded that Angelo was a "nice fellow," and, in a cascade of internal rhyme, decided that his trainer had "the connection and the complexion to get me the right protection which leads to good affection" (Torres 100).

A scant eight days after he arrived in Miami, Clay had his first fight with Dundee as his trainer. Cassius won against one Herb Siler in a 4th round technical knockout (TKO). As usual, he bragged at ringside that Floyd Patterson would soon feel his power. After knocking out Tony Esperti before his hometown Miami fans, Clay made news when he happened to run into Ingemar Johansson. The Swedish heavyweight champion was in town for a rematch with Patterson, whom he had pummeled in a stunning upset the previous year. Harold Conrad, the publicist for the Patterson–Johansson bout, was aware of Clay and his reputation for cockiness and thought that having Cassius spar with the champ might increase interest in the fight and ticket sales. The Louisville Lip was more than willing, quipping prior to the bout that he was ready to "go dancin' with Johansson" (Remnick 118).

The match, held on February 6, 1960, was one-sided from the beginning. Even though the Swedish champ had virtually destroyed Patterson, the 19-year-old Clay utterly befuddled him. The ponderous Ingemar couldn't even pretend to keep up with Cassius, who circled, flicked left jabs, didn't allow Johansson to land a solid punch, and taunted the older, heavier fighter with the ever-occurring mantra that he, Clay, should be the one to get in the ring with Patterson, not the Swede. Johansson's trainer, Whitey Bimstein, saw his fighter becoming increasingly frustrated and stopped the bout after two rounds. Cassius must not have been very extended by Johansson; on the next day he managed to knock out Jim Robinson, his next professional opponent, in the 1st round.

Although it wasn't an official fight, the two rounds with Johansson were especially important to Clay because a reporter for *Sports Illustrated* was in the audience. Gil Rogin was profoundly impressed with Cassius Clay. When he returned to the magazine's New York office, he told anyone who would listen that Clay was destined to be world champion. In

Rogin's view, it was "a lock" (Hauser 38). This began a symbiotic relationship between a magazine that would dominate the world of sports reporting and a fighter who would dominate his world as well.

Clay's next bout, two weeks later against Texan Donnie Fleeman, could have been a tough fight. Fleeman had 22 knockouts to his credit, including one over former champ Ezzard Charles. A supremely confident Clay nevertheless predicted a four-round knockout. Although Cassius opened cuts above both of his opponent's eyes, the referee let the bout go into the 7th round before mercifully ending it. Cassius then had his Louisville homecoming against Lamar Clark on April 18. Clark also should have put up more of a battle because he had knocked out 45 opponents in a row prior to this fight. Utterly unintimidated by this record, Clay predicted a 2nd round knockout. The referee stopped the bout in that very round, after Clay had broken his opponent's nose.

Under Dundee's tutelage, Cassius Clay had won convincingly six times and made a fool of the Heavyweight Champion of the World. He was having a ball. As his ringside doctor, Ferdie Pacheco put it, "Everything was such fun to him." Had an opponent been able to thump him good, perhaps he would have come down a bit. But, Percheco noted, "No one did. And so he just kept predicting a winning. It was like Candide; he didn't think anything bad could happen in this best of all possible worlds" (Remnick 119).

His next fight, however, would challenge this modern eternal optimist. He went to Las Vegas to take on Duke Sabedong, a 6'6" colossus from Hawaii. Clay was clearly the better fighter but was unable to put the giant away, winning only on points after 10 lackluster rounds. The Vegas trip did have one positive outcome, however, at least from the perspective of polishing Cassius's outrageous persona. He met the famed wrestler and showman, Gorgeous George, whose shtick made Clay look positively shy. While Cassius had merely predicted a victory over the Hawaiian, Gorgeous brought down the roof when he foresaw victory in his own next wrestling match: "I'll kill him! I'll tear his arm off! If this bum beats me, I'll crawl across the ring and cut my hair off." The wrestler advised the boxer to "keep on bragging, keep on sassing, and always be outrageous" (Remnick 120). Cassius was duly impressed, especially when a sold-out crowd began ranting at George. Cassius's outrageous mask had been confirmed by a master.

Clay went back to Louisville, where on July 22, 1961, he won another 10-round decision, this time against Alonzo Johnson, who was smart enough to stay away from Clay and at least finish the fight. The Johnson bout was significant because it marked a first: it was nationally televised on the Gillette Cavalcade of Sports, arranged by the Madison Square Garden official Teddy Brenner, whom Clay had previously charmed on his was to the Olympics. Brenner also organized Clay's next bout, against Alex Miteff, on October 7, 1961, a fight marred by the fact that no one had brought gloves. Officials managed to find two old pair "as hard as rocks," one of which Cassius used to knockout his opponent in the 6th round (Hauser 43). A month later, Clay scored a 7th-round knockout over Willie Besmanoff, another ranked heavyweight.[4]

Cassius Clay gained enormous confidence and renown in 1961. He drew increased media attention and perfected the combination of fighting skill and rhetorical flourishes that marked him as a real contender inside the ring and a character outside of it. Of course, he had numerous models for both his boxing style and personal charisma, ranging from Ray Robinson to Jack Johnson, and from his father to Gorgeous George. But Cassius was above all sui generis, his own creation. During that fabulous summer of 1961, he ran into some old friends who used to give him rides to the gym. They told him that they were among the many who had made him what he was and that he should remember them when he made his bundle. His father also tried to take credit for the creation of Cassius. The young Clay was willing to give him basic biological kudos, but as for what the 20-year-old phenomenon had become, he said, almost stirringly, "Who made me is *me*" (Remnick 121).

Part of Cassius's life seemed relatively unimportant at the time: his growing fascination with the Nation of Islam (NOI). The origins of this organization are clouded in myth, but we do know that in 1930, a black salesman who called himself Wali Farad Muhammad (born Wallace Fard) established what he called the Lost Found Nation of Islam in Detroit. His theology, although loosely Islamic, focused on explaining the oppression of African Americans while predicting their ultimate salvation. He preached, for example, that white people were actually inferior but devilishly clever beings created by an evil black scientist, Dr. Yacub. Whites were destined to rule the world until Allah sent psychic black supermen in planes to destroy the unrighteous (presumably whites) and raise blacks up to their naturally superior position. That time, W.F. Muhammad argued, would come soon.

Among his converts was Elijah Poole, a Georgia native who moved to Detroit to work on an automobile assembly line. He had been a member of Marcus Garvey's black nationalist movement in the 1920s and saw W. F. Muhammad as a powerful force for black liberation, especially when the leader claimed to be the final prophet of Allah. When W.F. Muhammad mysteriously disappeared in 1934, Elijah, who changed his name from

Poole to Muhammad, took over the Detroit mosque. Some 8,000 members, most of them quite poor and dispirited, found considerable meaning and hope in the NOI message. Following mainstream Islamic practice, the Nation called on its practitioners to lead a moral life, free of alcohol and sexual promiscuity, and to be decent and charitable people. In addition to a comforting theology and ethic, the Nation worked hard to provide some social welfare assistance for the black community.

Although Elijah Muhammad was arrested and jailed during World War II for encouraging resistance to the draft, he emerged after the war with a new plan for recruitment, based on his experience in prison. He believed that black convicts were largely ignored by African American Christian churches before, during, and after their jail time. Thus, he focused his search for new members on the downtrodden, including pimps, prostitutes, juvenile delinquents, hustlers, and convicts. Despite a dearth of accurate membership statistics, anecdotal evidence suggests a sustained growth in the late 1940s and 1950s, with new NOI mosques being opened in many major cities with large black populations.

The most important convert in the 1950s was Malcolm Little, a native Detroiter who moved to Boston and was imprisoned for burglary in 1946. Malcolm's brother, who had become a member of the NOI, discussed his new found religion with Malcolm, and after considerable study and reflection, in 1952 when he was paroled Malcolm Little became Malcolm X.[5] During the next decade, Malcolm was the most popular and visible NOI figure, as he became chief minister at mosques in Boston, New York, and Philadelphia. His speeches often focused on self-defense and opposition to the integration of blacks into white society. Indeed, he saw whites as "blue-eyed devils" with whom no self-respecting black person would want to integrate. His charismatic preaching was no doubt responsible for much of the religion's success, as its membership grew from around 500 in 1952 to more than 30,000 in 1963. It was an especially popular and potent force in black areas such as Harlem, primarily because it both gave African Americans a sense of identity and helped alleviate problems associated with poverty and aimlessness. As black memoirist Claude Brown recalled, "It made [members] feel as though they had something," especially ex-prisoners, drug addicts, and prostitutes who used the faith to turn their lives around (Brown 332).[6]

When he first heard about the NOI in Chicago in 1959, Cassius apparently met some Muslims in their south-side homes. One of his aunts recalls that he returned to Louisville after a Golden Gloves tournament in Chicago with a recording of some of Elijah Muhammad's sermons. Clay also apparently read the official NOI newspaper, *Muhammad Speaks*, and tried, unsuccessfully, to convince one of his high school teachers to let him write a term paper on the group. After winning his Olympic gold medal, he went to meetings of various civil rights groups, including the National Association for the Advancement of Colored People (NAACP) and the Congress for Racial Equality (CORE).[7] But he was always most impressed by what he heard in several Muslim mosques. David Remnick speculates that the young Cassius, with memories of Emmett Till and numerous racial slights and wounds from his own childhood in Louisville, found in the NOI "something that had resonated in his mind, something about the discipline and bearing of the Muslims, their sense of hierarchy, manhood, and self-respect, the way they refused to smoke or drink or carouse, their racial pride" (Remnick 127).

In March 1961, shortly after he arrived in Miami to work with Angelo Dundee, Cassius met Abdul Rahaman, a former self-styled "sportsman" who converted to the NOI and was sent by Elijah Muhammad to proselytize for the faith. He took Cassius to the local mosque, where the young fighter was captivated. Clay recalls that "the first time I ever felt spiritual in my life was when [I] walked in that Muslim temple in Miami." He was entranced when one speaker attacked the common usage of "Negro" to characterize African Americans: "If you see a Canadian coming, you know he's from Canada. What country is called Negro?" (Hauser 90). Clay was so impressed that he began reading *Muhammad Speaks* every week, continued talking to NOI members, and began thinking long and hard about his spiritual life. He also came to the attention of Jeremiah Shabazz, the chief Muslim minister in the South, who traveled from Atlanta to meet and instruct the potential recruit. Clay was like a sponge, soaking up the wisdom of Malcolm X, who criticized nonviolent civil rights advocates such as peaceful sit-in demonstrators: "A coward can sit... . It takes a real man to stand." Shabazz emphasized the doctrine of self defense, again quoting Malcolm, who warned that instead of turning the other cheek to violent whites, blacks should proudly say, "Put your hands on us...and we'll put you to death" (Remnick 129). Clay, who saw blacks as the victims of white hatred, responded positively to the NOI rhetoric. Shabazz also caused Cassius to reexamine his concept of the physical Jesus, which, of course, had been based largely on paintings that portrayed Him as white: "Who said Jesus was white?" Cassius wondered. "What painter ever saw Jesus?" (Ali, *Butterfly* 65).

In late 1961 Rahaman became a hanger-on at the 5th Street Gym, and soon Shabazz supplied Cassius with a Muslim cook so the young fighter could more easily obey the Islamic dietary regimen. In early 1962, Clay went to Detroit where he met both Elijah Muhammad and Malcolm X.

He was profoundly impressed: Elijah Muhammad was a "good man" who tried to "lift up" black Americans, while Malcolm "was very intelligent, with a good sense of humor, a wise man" (Hauser 97). Even though Elijah disapproved of prizefighting, Malcolm X, his most influential minister, sought out Clay once he learned that he was a strong contender for the heavyweight title. Malcolm found Clay to be a "likable, friendly, clean cut youngster" who was smart enough to try to goad Sonny Liston into a title bout in which the champ would be "angry, poorly trained, and over-confident" (Remnick 165). The two became mentor and mentee, a rela-tionship that would have a profound impact on Clay's life. Cassius Clay was clearly on his way to becoming Muhammad Ali.

The year 1962 also saw Clay further mature as a fighter. Between February and July, he won five bouts, all by knockouts and none lasting more than six rounds. In September, he took time out from his training to attend the Floyd Patterson–Sonny Liston heavyweight championship bout in Chicago's Comiskey Park. Fighting Patterson for the title had been Clay's goal since his days as an amateur, but a powerful Liston anni-hilated the champ in the 1st round. Clay seemed unimpressed, as he launched another bit of doggerel after the bout: "When people left the Park/You could hear them say 'Liston will remain the king/Until he meets Cassius Clay.'" Liston's response when Cassius taunted him after the fight was an ominous "You're next loudmouth" (Cottrell 79).

But their confrontation in the ring would not come for another year and a half. Clay looked to the task of taking on his most formidable oppo-nent since sparring with Ingemar Johansson in early 1961—Archie Moore—in October 1962. Dundee saw Clay's bout with his ageless former mentor as a step up, at least in terms of an opponent with name recogni-tion. No one seriously thought Moore had much of a chance, and Moore admitted that he agreed to the fight for purely financial reasons. But in spite of considerable hype, including the inevitable ragging by Clay, tick-ets moved slowly, and the confrontation was postponed until November 15. Moore complained to the promoter's wife: "You mean another three weeks of listening to him shoot his mouth off?" Cassius shot back with a poetic offering that predicted that Moore would be finished in the 4th round (Torres 112). Clay's prediction was accurate, as Moore fell in four, mainly, he claimed, because Cassius hit him so many times on the top of the head that he became dizzy. Moore concluded that the young fighter "would have beaten Joe Louis four times out of five" (Hauser 49). And, significantly, the famed light heavyweight believed that Cassius Clay was "definitely ready for heavyweight champion [Sonny] Liston" (Remnick 124).

But the young man from Louisville had work to do before he would fight Liston. Cassius easily defeated Charlie Powell in three rounds in January 1963, but his next fight against Doug Jones in New York City proved surprisingly difficult. He thought that Jones, whom he outweighed by 14 pounds, would be a pushover. Clay complained that a newspaper strike in New York would deprive hero-starved citizens of the Big Apple of the thrill of seeing stories about his triumph. He even participated in a poetry reading in Greenwich Village, in which he compared himself favorably to his Roman namesakes, Marcellus sacker of Carthage and Cassius sacker of Julius Caesar, concluding that when he beat Jones he would take the mantle as "the noblest Roman of them all" (Remnick 136).

Fans so eagerly anticipated the bout, according to Robert Cassidy, that "for the first time in its history, Madison Square Garden was sold out two days before an event." Jones fought brilliantly, however, using his speed and finesse to slip most of Clay's punches, and lasted all ten rounds, even rocking him with a hard right in the 1st round. Although Cassius won a unanimous decision, the two judges scored the bout only 5-4-1 for Clay. Cassidy notes that "when the decision was announced, the crowd...began to chant, 'Fix! Fix!'" (Cassidy 30, 31). On leaving the ring, Cassius grumbled, "I ain't Superman" (Remnick 139). Perhaps in part because of the controversy, *The Ring Magazine* named the bout the fight of the year for 1963. The lead-up to the contest had one unalloyed positive outcome for Clay: he met Drew "Bundini" Brown—a black convert to Judaism whose name for God was "Shorty" and who had an innate capacity to make Cassius laugh. They became inseparable for most of Clay's career.[8]

His next fight, against British heavyweight Henry Cooper on June 18, 1963, featured a huge crowd—55,000 people in London's Wembley Stadium—and a vicious blow that knocked Clay flat in the 4th round. After Dundee got his fighter some extra time by enlarging a rip in one of his gloves between rounds, Cassius pummeled Cooper for a TKO in the predicted 5th round. After the bout, Clay claimed that Cooper snuck in the blow that felled him while his attention was diverted by the gorgeousness of actress Elizabeth Taylor, who was sitting ringside. But some boxing aficionados, including Senator Estes Kefauver, saw the Cooper fight as another example of Clay's lack of prizefighting savvy. The Tennessee Democrat intoned to reporters that "it would be 'many years' before Cassius Clay was mature enough to take on the champion."[9] The Senator's opinion aside, after the Cooper fight, Jack Nilon, Sonny Liston's manager, appeared in Clay's dressing room to deliver a message: "I've flown three thousand miles to tell you we're ready" (Remnick 140, 141).

Although no official papers were signed until several months later, the first step had been taken. The Louisville Lip would face the terrible Sonny Liston in a battle that almost everyone but Cassius Clay thought he would lose.

NOTES

1. Clay took an extra precaution on the flight by wearing a parachute purchased at an army surplus store. "My plan was to drop to the floor as soon as the plane started shaking, so I could jump out and pull the cord" (Ali, *Butterfly*, 34).

2. Privately, however, Cassius was less sanguine. Indeed, he recalls thinking as the U.S. national anthem was played that as champion he might "be able to do something for my people." Naively he believed that he would even "get equality for [them]" (Ali, *Butterfly* 34).

3. In his autobiography, *The Greatest*, Cassius alleges that he and a friend were denied service at a Louisville restaurant shortly after he returned from the Olympic Games, even though his friend showed the owner the gold medal. They were then hassled and almost severely beaten by a white racist motorcycle gang whose leader wanted the gold medal to give to his girlfriend. After a nearly miraculous escape, Cassius claims that he was so disillusioned by continuing white racism that he threw his medal into the Ohio River, as he shouted to his friend, "We don't need it" (Ali, *Greatest* 77). In 1998, David Remnick claimed that although this story is powerful, it is untrue. It was included in the autobiography at the insistence of Cassius's Nation of Islam handlers, who wanted him to emphasize the effects of white racism on his psyche. According to Remnick, there was no motorcycle gang and "Clay did not throw away his medal, he lost it" (Remnick 89). The final word in this dispute belongs to Cassius. In his recent memoir, *The Soul of a Butterfly*, Cassius admits that "over the years" he had "told some people" that he had lost the medal. However, the story he told in *The Greatest* was essentially true. Although he says nothing about a motorcycle gang in *Butterfly*, he does say of the gold medal: "The world should know the truth— it's somewhere at the bottom of the Ohio River" (Ali, *Butterfly* 41).

4. Cassius had predicted a 7th-round knockout of Besmanoff but could have finished him off much sooner. Despite Dundee's pleas to end the torture, Cassius carried his opponent until the appointed round.

5. NOI members usually replaced their last names with "X" because they saw their regular surnames as "slave names." The "X" symbolized the lost African tribal name.

6. While a graduate student at Columbia University in the early 1960s, this author took the wrong subway line and inadvertently wandered into a Malcolm X rally. His speech was so mesmerizing that I began to cheer and chant with the

crowd, until I noticed that I was the only "blue-eyed devil" in sight. I walked quickly toward my dormitory.

7. The NAACP and CORE were two major civil rights organizations during this period, both pushing for racial integration.

8. Also in 1963, Cassius recorded an album of his poetry, entitled "I Am the Greatest." Noted American poet Marianne Moore, who had become a great fan of Clay's poetry, actually wrote the liner notes.

9. Kefauver failed to note how bloodied Cooper was in the four or so rounds that he managed to stay conscious. The British press liked to say that Cooper had "a great capacity for human suffering" (Cosell 183).

Chapter 4

THE LISTON BOUTS AND THE "TOTAL ECLIPSES OF THE SONNYS": JUNE 1964–MAY 1965

When Jack Nilon flew to London to do a deal with Clay's people after the Cooper fight, Cassius had just about perfected his initial persona. The result of both his natural ebullience and a calculated effort to generate publicity, the Cassius Clay that the world saw was a wise-cracking, loud mouthed braggart who taunted his opponents outside and inside the ring and tossed about round-predicting doggerel at the drop of a hat. As we have seen, being lippy was a marvelous way to draw crowds and bigger purses to his bouts, thereby paving his way to a large share of the American dream.

By this time, Clay's fighting style had also solidified. He used his great speed and fancy footwork to dance around his opponents as he flicked telling jabs and powerful counter punches. But his sluggish ten-round decision over Doug Jones and knock down by Henry Cooper caused most observers of the sport to wonder if he was really ready for Liston. Certainly Nilon saw the fight as easy money for the champion (Remnick 141). The Liston entourage decided there was no better fighter around than Cassius and that Clay's mouth would help generate a large crowd, while his body could not stand the champ's powerful blows. Sonny Liston was an animal who would devour the young challenger.

No contemporary African American fighters had more contrasting backgrounds than Cassius Clay and Sonny Liston. Clay's relatively middle-class upbringing in a small nuclear family emphasized classic American values. On the other hand, Charles "Sonny" Liston was born into a blended family that eventually included 25 children. His father, Tobe Liston, was 50 when he married Helen, age 16, who became Sonny's natural mother. Tobe removed Sonny from school at the age of eight to help in the fields as the family tried to scratch out a living as sharecroppers in Arkansas. Hoping for a modicum of economic advancement, his mother took some of her children to St. Louis, leaving Sonny to the tender mercies of a father who beat him so often that when he skipped a day, Sonny wondered what he could have possibly done right to avoid a beating. When he was 13, Sonny fled his father to join Helen, and within three years grew in both physical stature—at 16 he was more than six feet tall and tipped the scales at more than 200 pounds—and in his fascination with a life of crime. He tried honest work: "I sold coal. I sold ice. I sold wood." But his family could not make ends meet. He recalled that "on the good days I ate. On the bad ones, I told my stomach to forget it" (McRae 307). So he turned to the streets. After a series of petty thefts and muggings, Sonny was convicted in 1950 of armed robbery and sentenced to five years in prison. Under the aegis of the prison chaplain, Father Alois Stevens, who recognized Sonny's skill, he began a formal boxing regimen, which led to his winning the prison's heavyweight championship. In 1952, Father Stevens helped convince the parole board to let Liston out early. Within a few months, he was winning Golden Gloves bouts, and in 1953 he joined the professional ranks.

Liston was fast out of the gate; he won 18 of his first 19 fights. Unfortunately, however, he became involved with local mobster John Vitale, who used the hulking ex-convict to keep his black workers in line. Liston said that this connection caused him to be harassed constantly by the St. Louis police and led ultimately to an assault conviction in 1956 when an officer claimed Sonny had pistol whipped him. Released in early 1958, Liston went back into the ring, where his prowess drew the attention of an even more powerful mobster, Frankie Carbo, who bought 52 percent of his contract and hired flunky managers. Seemingly oblivious to the criminal element in his corner, during the next four years, Liston simply destroyed his opposition. He won 15 fights, 13 by knockouts, nine of which came in the first three rounds. Then, in 1962 he destroyed champion Floyd Patterson in one round and repeated the feat when he defended his title in 1963.

As he had with the first Patterson–Liston fight, Cassius showed up for the reprise in Las Vegas in July 1963 and taunted the champ unmercifully. The Liston camp had not yet officially offered Clay a shot at the title, so, according to Harold Conrad, a public relations expert who knew both Clay and Liston, Cassius launched a campaign to goad the champ into fighting him. He barged into Liston's training camp and told Sonny that he couldn't even beat a nonfighting member of his entourage, Jack

McKinney. Later he ran into Liston rolling dice in a casino and shouted out, "Look at that big ugly bear, he can't even shoot craps," to which Sonny responded, "If you don't get out of here in ten seconds, I'm going to pull that big tongue out of your mouth and stick it up your ass." He then proceeded to slap Clay in the face. The young challenger was stunned, having assumed that Liston had the sense to see the taunting as a form of gate-building (Remnick 74). Clay obviously recovered from his shock quickly enough. A few days later at the fight, as tradition demand-ed, former champs and current contenders were introduced to the crowd prior to the 1st round. Clay strutted around the ring to resounding boos. To Joe Louis, who was also in the ring, Cassius was like "a demented puppy who kept pissing on the floor" trying "desperately to get noticed" (McRae 309).[1] Immediately after Liston knocked out Patterson, Cassius leaped into the ring, screaming, "Liston's a tramp! I'm the champ" and "Don't make me wait. I'll whip him in eight." Sonny didn't seem worried. Later, when asked by a reporter how long the fight with Clay would last, Liston coldly responded, "Two rounds—one and a half to catch him and, and a half round to lick him" (Remnick 77).

Clay's antics paid off. On November 5, 1963, papers were signed for a February 1964 championship bout in Miami Beach. Interestingly, the Louisville Sponsoring Group thought that Clay wasn't ready. One of the group's lawyers, Gordon Davidson, concluded that Cassius didn't "care about becoming one of the finest heavyweights who ever lived. All he wants to be is the richest" (Hauser 60). Nonetheless, the stage had been set for a grudge battle that the participants hoped would fill the stands and the nation's sports pages.

The fight was promoted by Florida businessman William MacDonald, a kind of mirror image of Cassius Clay's dream to become wealthy and world famous. MacDonald, a self-proclaimed descendent of Montana sheep rustlers, worked his way up from being a conductor on a bus to a millionaire who promoted fights for fun. He was wise enough to realize that for the gate to grow, people needed to think Cassius had a chance to win, and so he predicted a Clay victory. As David Remnick observed, "You don't sell tickets when David has no shot a Goliath" (Remnick 146). And, of course, the official promoter had a great deal of help from boxing's greatest unofficial self-promoter since Jack Johnson.

Cassius went wild. Indeed, later in his career, he claimed that he was "crazy" during this period. But similar to Hamlet, he was largely feigning that madness, because, as always, he knew the value of hype in prying money from fight fans. His mouth also became part of his boxing strategy. He conjectured that if he relentlessly hounded Liston verbally, the champ, in Clay's words, would get so mad that, when the fight came, "he'd try to kill me and forget everything he knew about boxing" (Hauser 60).

The pre-bout needling continued seemingly without pause. Cassius went so far as to meet Liston's plane when it landed in Miami. As Sonny walked down the steps, Clay rushed up to him screaming, "Chump! Big ugly bear! I'm gonnna whup you right now." He even followed Liston's car from the airport. Sonny became so upset that he ordered the car to stop, jumped out, and ran toward Clay, who had emerged from his own vehicle: "Listen you little punk," Liston exploded, "I'll punch you in the mouth. This has gone too far." Clay took off his jacket, shouting his own insults, "Come on chump. Right here." At that point, members of the respective retinues separated the two (Remnick 173, 174). But Sonny had gotten a clear indication of the digs and verbal jousts he was in for. Some examples during the weeks preceding the bout: "Whop! Whop! Bop! Bop! I'll make him look so bad they'll call it a mismatch"; "I'm young, I'm handsome, I'm fast. I can't possibly be beat. And if he don't want to fight, he should keep his ugly self at home that night"; "If it wasn't for me, the fight game would be dead" (Hauser 60, 61, 62). And, inevitably, the poetic prediction. Only this one was no couplet or quatrain. Perhaps because of the significance of the occasion, Clay drew on all his muses to pen a 33-line mini epic, with a conceit that would make John Donne (a seventeenth-century English poet) take notice. Cassius imagines that he hits Sonny so hard that the champ is lofted out of the ring and into the heavens where he becomes a veritable Sputnik-like satellite. The fortunate crowd will have witnessed a "total eclipse of the Sonny!" (Hauser 62).

Here, Cassius Clay, similar to a hero in the Trojan War, seems godlike in his prowess as he sends his opponent toward heaven but certainly with no heavenly reward for the orbiting ex-champion. So powerful is young Clay that his Liston launch defies scientific law, somehow turning Sonny into both a satellite and an eclipse. All wonderful fun that no doubt brought smiles to the faces of millions.

Sonny Liston, however, was not one of those who chuckled at Clay's antics. His responses to the verbal jibes were terse and only feebly comic: "My only worry is how I'll get my fist outta his big mouth once I get him in the ring"; or more simply and ominously, "I might hurt that boy bad" (Hauser 60).

Most sports pundits thought that Liston's predictions were more viable than Clay's, including the dean of American sports writers, Jimmy Cannon of the *New York Journal-American*. Cannon, who had written about sports since 1936, idolized Joe Louis and saw Clay as the Brown

Bomber's polar opposite.[2] Louis had about him what Cannon called a "barbaric majesty." Clay was merely a showman, "all pretense and gas....No honesty....a freak, a bantamweight who weighs 200 pounds." While watching Clay train for the bout, Cannon concluded that he could "never get away" with his hands down, gliding, leaning away style with Liston (Remnick 151). Young reporter Robert Lypsyte, who got to cover the fight when the regular *New York Times* boxing writer decided that it would be boring, believed that Cannon feared Clay because the fighter didn't "know his place" the way Joe Louis did. "The idea that he was a loud braggart brought disrespect to this noble sport....Clay lacked dignity" (Remnick 157). To Cannon, he wasn't a good prizefighter or a "good Negro." Other boxing pundits agreed completely with Cannon. Journalist Robert Boyle concluded that Clay "must be kidding" to want to get into the ring with a "deadly fighting machine." His colleague Arthur Daley wrote that Cassius "can't fight as well as he can talk." According to reporter Tex Maule, Clay's jab merely "stings" but Liston's "wounds." Correspondent Milton Gross summed up the dominant opinion of experts about the fight. It was nothing more than "soap bubble promotion." Although Cassius "knows publicity and is a charmer," he "doesn't know [the] business" of boxing, a fact that would become clear when Liston did "a butchery job on his pretty face" (Hauser 67, 68, 69). Even comedians jumped at the chance to cop a laugh at Clay's expense. Joe E. Lewis quipped that he "was betting on Clay—to live," while Jackie Gleason chimed in, "Clay should last about 18 seconds and that includes the three seconds he brings in the ring with him." Even Joe Louis, the great former champ (who was part of the Liston entourage), couldn't believe Clay's patter. Louis said, simply, "He's got to be kidding" (Torres 135).[3]

Clay may well have agreed with these detractors on some level. He admitted that Liston was "scary" (Hauser 60). When asked by reporter Mort Sharnik if he believed he could defeat Liston, Clay compared himself to Christopher Columbus who had faith that the world was round. He even asked Liston's manager, Jack Nilon, to give him $10,000 to "provision" a get away bus in case he lost on his "day of reckoning" (Remnick 150).

In public, however, Cassius was basically having a ball. In one of the most newsworthy prefight stories, promoter MacDonald's chief public relations man, Harold Conrad, actually arranged a meeting between Clay and the wildly popular musical group, the Beatles. A week before the bout, the Fab Four were in Miami Beach to appear on the Ed Sullivan Show, one of the most popular shows on television at the time. Conrad also took Liston to the show to plug the fight. When they were backstage observing the group, Sonny grumbled, "Are these the m————s what all the people are screaming about? My dog plays drums better than that kid with the big nose" (Hauser 63). When Conrad took the Beatles to the 5th Street Gym, Clay was nowhere to be seen. The impatient Beatles tried to leave, but two burly state troopers blocked their exit. Clay finally sauntered in, told the boys that he'd like to join them in road shows, and then mock punched them to the canvas with what he labeled his "domino punch." When he jokingly said that they weren't as dumb as they looked, John Lennon, tongue in cheek, replied, "No, but you are" (Remnick 158). The Beatles and Cassius parted, chuckling at their ability to put on a show.[4]

Other, more portentous events were occurring outside the ring prior to the bout. Cassius was moving closer to the Nation of Islam, and the press was beginning to notice. Clay later admitted that he had been going to NOI meetings since 1961 but, said that he would "sneak through the back door" because he feared that he "wouldn't be allowed to fight for the title" if the press learned of his growing commitment to a group scorned and feared by most Americans (Hauser 97). Despite his caution, however, on September 1963, two months before the contract for the fight was signed, a Philadelphia newspaper reported that Clay had attended a local Black Muslim rally. On January 21, 1964, he left his training camp, accompanied by Black Muslim minister Malcolm X, to speak at an NOI gathering in New York City. *The New York Herald Tribune* picked up the story and called Clay "the first nationally prominent Negro to take an active part in the Muslim movement." The paper did note, however, that Cassius had "not formally announced support for the Muslims" (Hauser 64). A few days later, the *Louisville Courier Journal* featured a story in which Cassius praised the Black Muslims and condemned the concept of racial integration. Then, on February 7, a few days before the scheduled bout, the *Miami Herald* ran a story in which Clay's father claimed that his son had become a member of the NOI and would announce that fact and a change from his "slave" name after the Liston fight.

As the Clay–Muslim connection gathered steam in the press, MacDonald went ballistic. He was convinced that white southerners, always sensitive to racial issues, would shun the bout once they realized that Clay was cozying up to what they perceived as black extremists. MacDonald was especially upset by the fact that Malcolm X was in Miami Beach as a part of the Clay entourage. In fact, Cassius paid for a hotel room for Malcolm, his pregnant wife Betty, and their three daughters and saw Malcolm virtually every day.[5] The promoter was convinced that the

Muslim connection would ruin the gate and any chance of his financially breaking even. Three days before the fight, he demanded that Clay
deny any ties to the NOI, which Cassius adamantly refused to do: "My
religion is more important to me than the fight," Clay remembered telling
MacDonald, at which point the promoter said that the fight was off.
Publicist Harold Conrad brokered a last minute compromise. Realizing
that MacDonald saw Malcolm's presence as the chief impediment, he
urged the Muslim leader to ostentatiously leave town until the day of the
fight. Malcolm agreed, MacDonald relented, and the bout was back
on—as was the hype.

Cassius raised that hype to a new level at the weigh-in on the morning
of the fight. Dundee and Sugar Ray Robinson, a member of his entourage,
warned Cassius to behave himself. After all, a heavyweight championship
weigh-in should be a serious, even solemn occasion. Clay, however, had
his own ideas. Arriving well before Liston, the challenger went berserk.
He and chief court jester Bundini Brown began screaming, "Float like a
butterfly, sting like a bee." Cassius then began beating a walking stick on
the floor, demanding that Sonny show up ready to move up the bout to
the weigh-in. When Liston still didn't appear, Clay and his people moved
to a dressing room to wait because fight officials threatened to fine
Cassius if he continued his outrageous behavior. He emerged a few minutes later, and Liston appeared shortly after. Clay reprised his act, lunging
toward Sonny, almost gurgling, "I'm gonna eat you alive," as William
Faversham of the Louisville Sporting Group tried to restrain him. The
ceremony devolved into near chaos, as, in the words of reporter Mort
Sharnik, seemingly everyone was "screaming and shoving and jockeying
for better camera angles, and Cassius was probably having a ball." If so,
he would pay for it. Morris Klein, chairman of the Miami Boxing
Commission, announced that Cassius would be fined $2,500, and
Alexander Robbins, the Commission physician, noted that Clay's pulse
was raging at 110 beats a minute, double its normal rate. Almost inciden-
tal to the brouhaha was the fact that Cassius weighed in at 210 pounds,
eight fewer than Sonny (Hauser 69, 70).[6]

Was Cassius Clay literally frightened into temporary insanity? The ring
doctor and members of the boxing commission certainly thought such a
condition was possible. Robbins said that Clay was "emotionally unbal-
anced, scared to death, and liable to crack up before he enters the ring"
(Hauser 71). Commission members then ordered Clay's doctor to continue to monitor the challenger's pulse. As Ferdie Pacheco later reported,
miraculously, within a hour of the weigh-in, Clay's pulse was back to
normal. When he asked Cassius why he had behaved so irrationally, Clay

said, simply, so that "Liston [will think] I'm a nut. He is scared of no man, but he is scared of a nut. Now he doesn't know what I am going to do" (Remnick 182).[7]

Cassius took a nap after his pulse went back to normal, seemingly oblivious to the possibility of defeat. His manager, Angelo Dundee, was also optimistic, convinced that the faster Clay would wear Liston down. Pacheco was less sanguine; in fact, he spent much of that prefight afternoon figuring out the best route to the closest hospital. When the Clay retinue arrived at the arena, they were disappointed to see that it was just half full. Only 8,297 tickets had been sold at the almost 16,000-seat venue. Clay and the Louisville group split $630,000—Liston received $1.3 million—while promoter MacDonald took a $300,000 soaking. He was never able to repeat the "Good Negro–Bad Negro" appeal of the popular Patterson–Liston fights. As David Remnick astutely observed, "For most Caucasian Floridians (and who else had the money to pay for a seat?) this was a matchup between a Muslim punk and a terrifying thug" (Remnick 185).

Cassius watched from the back of an aisle as his younger brother, Rudy, fought in the first preliminary bout. When he barely won, Cassius consoled his brother by putting him in charge of his water bottle. According to biographer John Tessitore, Cassius was afraid that "Liston's friends in organized crime would attempt to poison him" (Tessitore 43). Clearly, the challenger was nervous. There were none of the crazy high jinks of the morning weigh-in. Cassius sat fidgeting in his dressing room; shortly before he was to enter the stadium, he, Rudy, and Malcolm, after figuring out which direction was east, prayed to Allah. At the same time, Liston's dressing room exuded calm. One of his corner men recalled that "as much as Clay got under Sonny's skin, we all believed the night would turn out okay." Before leaving for the ring, Sonny donned his traditional robe, with its hood pulled over his head—the "executioner's robe," according to another member of his entourage (Remnick 188). At 10:00 P.M., Cassius Clay entered the ring for the most crucial fight of his young career. The "executioner" followed a few seconds later.

When referee Barney Felix gave the traditional instructions, Liston fixed Clay with a baleful stare. Later, Cassius admitted that he was sacred at that moment: "It frightened me, just knowing how hard he hit" (Hauser 74). But the taller Clay had the presence of mind to stare back—and *down*—at Sonny, establishing "a point of information." At the end of the referee's instructions, Clay spoke to Liston for the first time since they entered the ring: "I've got you now, sucker" (Remnick 189, 190).[8] When the fighters came out at the bell, Liston threw the first punch, "a left jab that missed by a foot" (Torres 136). Clay recalls that in that 1st round he danced around, avoiding Liston's power, and even landed a few combination punches. After round one, Clay says, "I felt good because I knew I could survive" (Hauser 75).

Jose Torres remembers the 2nd round as a kind of subliminal turning point. Clay didn't especially hurt Liston, in fact, the champ cornered his challenger on the ropes and seemed for a second ready to pounce. But, as Torres notes, "Clay slipped out without trouble and a roar went up from the crowd" (Torres 136).[9] Mort Sharnik saw the 3rd round as the key to the fight. For the first time, Cassius took the fight to Sonny—jabs, combination punches, straight right hands. To Sharnik, "it was like the armor plate on a battleship being pierced." It struck the Miami reporter at that moment that Liston was not indestructible. When he saw a bruise beneath the champ's right eye, he told himself, "My God, Cassius Clay is winning this fight" (Hauser 75).

During round 4, Clay mainly coasted, but near the end of the round an event occurred that is still the subject of enormous controversy. Cassius started having difficulty seeing; after the bell ended the round, he came to his corner in obvious pain, shouting, "I can't see! My eyes!" He pleaded with Dundee, "Cut the gloves off, we're going home" (Hauser 75). Clearly some substance had gotten into his eyes and was causing excruciating pain. Dundee hypothesized that Clay had somehow gotten some of the liniment put on Liston's cuts on his glove, then inadvertently rubbed his glove near one of his eyes. Reporter Jack McKinney tells a more sinister story. He claims that one of Liston's corner men, Joe Pollino, told him after the fight that between rounds 3 and 4, Liston instructed him "to juice the gloves," that is, apply a stinging liniment that could damage Clay's vision.[10] Whatever the cause of the extreme irritation, Dundee stood firm, screamed "bullshit" when Clay wanted to quit, sponged water in his fighter's eyes, and told him to go out in the fifth and keep away from Sonny until his vision improved. Clay obeyed, and by the middle of the 5th round, his vision had cleared, and the challenger stayed in the fight. In the sixth, Cassius went on the offensive. A series of jabs, counter punches, and upper cuts left Liston reeling. Clay recalls, "I hit him with eight punches in a row, until he doubled up. I remember thinking something like, 'Yeah, you old sucker. You try to be so big and bad'" (Remnick 198). Two left hooks near the end of the round almost put Sonny to the canvas.

Then the unexpected happened. As Clay walked to his corner, "arms and mouth open," in the words of Jose Torres, Liston told his manager, "That's it" (Torres 139; Remnick 199). Liston refused to emerge from his corner. The fight was over, one round earlier than the Louisville Lip had predicted, one of the greatest upsets in boxing history. Naturally, Cassius Clay became a whirling dervish. He jumped, leapt, and waved his arms. He stood still long enough to stare at the press row, at Jimmy Cannon, and at all those who predicted his defeat and scream, wild-eyed: "I am the king! I am the king! King of the world. Eat your words. Eat your words." And journalist Red Smith did, writing the next day in response to Clay's mantra, "And nobody ever had a better right [to say what Cassius said]." Significantly, among Clay's torrent of words were the following: "Almighty God was with me!" and "I talk to God every day"—words that would soon mean much more than a tired sports ritual praising the Lord. Cassius Clay, soon to be Cassius X, then Muhammad Ali, really meant what he said (Remnick 200).

Both fighters talked to reporters after the bout. Sonny was alternately philosophical and disconsolate. At one point, he said that losing the championship was "one of those little things that happened to you." Close to tears, no doubt, he then said that losing "made him 'feel like when the President got shot'" (Torres 138–39). Taken to a local hospital as a precaution, Liston "looked like a middle-aged truck driver who had driven into an abutment," according to reporter Mort Sharnik (Remnick 202).

When Clay talked about Liston, he was unusually subdued. He chided the media for "[building] him up too big," which meant he had "such a long way to fall" (Torres 139). Then, the new champ berated the press, daring them to call him anything other that the Greatest. Media representatives realized now that in the run up to the fight Clay had been dead right. As one reporter observed, "They sent a boy to do a man's job—and he did it" (Torres 139). The manchild then went back to his hotel room, ate some ice cream, talked with his friend and mentor Malcolm X, and the great Cleveland Browns running back, Jim Brown, then fell asleep—significantly in Malcolm's bed—a strange foreshadowing of the revelation he would make the next morning.

The day-after-the-fight press conference started innocently enough, with stock questions about the match. Clay claimed that he didn't really like to fight, that he wanted to set an example to little children, to be "a nice clean gentleman." Then a reporter asked him directly if he was a "card-carrying member of the Black Muslims" (Remnick 205). Clay objected to the term "card carrying" but admitted that he was no longer a Christian. He now believed in Allah.[11] As a member of the Nation of Islam, he would become to most whites and some blacks a different kind of, but equally menacing threat as Jack Johnson in the early twentieth century and Sonny Liston in the 1950s and 1960s.

In a follow-up interview the next day, Clay and Malcolm elaborated on the champion's conversion. Cassius wanted to be called Cassius X and condemned the press's euphemism, Black Muslims. Malcolm X crowed that Cassius would be more important to his people than any other black athlete including Jackie Robinson. In Chicago, Elijah Muhammad, who had been ambivalent about too close a relationship between the NOI and professional athletics, came fully on board, praising Cassius and claiming that Allah had made his victory possible. Two weeks after the public conversion, Elijah gave Cassius X a new name. While most members of the Nation changed their "slave" names by replacing their surname with an "X," Elijah granted Cassius the signal honor of a "completed" Muslim name, usually reserved for long-standing members of the NOI. Elijah embraced the prizefighter by naming him Muhammad Ali.[12]

Reaction to Ali's conversion came swiftly and was largely negative. Although his immediate handlers like Angelo Dundee claimed they didn't care what their fighter's religion was, most observers were stunned.[13] Ali's father maintained that the Black Muslims had "conned" his son and said that he, the senior Cassius Marcellus Clay, would proudly continue to use the name, maybe even "make money out of it" (Torres 147–48). White reporters had a field day. Jimmy Cannon encapsulated the rage most white sportswriters felt when he fulminated that Ali's membership in the NOI had turned boxing "into an instrument of mass hate" (Hauser 104). Boxing officials were also upset. Ed Lassman, president of the World Boxing Association (WBA), claimed that "Clay is a detriment to the boxing world... and is setting a poor example for the youth of the world" (Torres 149). He suspended Ali, but the ruling had little effect because major state boxing commissions ignored it. When Ali went to watch a colleague's bout in New York on March 20, 1964, Harry Markson, president of Madison Square Garden, refused to allow the champ's new name to be announced; when "Cassius Clay" boomed from the PA system, Ali stormed out to a chorus of boos. Members of the Louisville Sponsoring Group were also upset and feared for their investment. Lawyer Gordon Davidson worried that "the Muslims would want to control things on their own"—a prophetic concern (Remnick 210). One of the few prominent whites who approved of Ali's conversion was Senator Richard Russell (D-Ga.). A rabid segregationist he warmly praised the NOI's opposition to racial integration and defended Ali's decision on the Senate floor.[14]

It was the NOI's stance on segregation that bothered some black newspapers when Ali converted. Frank Stanley of the *Louisville Defender*, for example, said the champ could join whatever religion he wanted but was "dismayed at [his] disassociation from the desegregation movement." Martin Luther King Jr. agreed, advising "Clay," as he continued to call him, to "spend more time proving his boxing skill and do less talking" (Remnick 211).[15] Black prizefighters joined in the criticism. Joe Louis believed that Cassius had let down the public when he joined the NOI, while Floyd Patterson actually sent him a written note, daring him to step in the ring. Like Louis, Patterson believed that the Black Muslims were un–American and offered to fight in the name of "all the people who think and feel as I do" (Torres 148).[16]

Ali naturally thought his critics were ill-informed. When he heard that the WBA had suspended him, he shot back, "That's [the] one way you might get me whupped," then proceeded to defend himself as "clean and peaceful." He responded to Joe Louis by calling him "a sucker," while his natural puckishness resurfaced when he answered Floyd Patterson's challenge: "I'll play with him for ten rounds. He has been talking about my religion. I will just pow him. Then after I beat him I'll convert him" (Torres 149).

In a more reflective mood, Ali talked to a reporter from *Boxing and Wrestling* magazine about his faith and its relation to black and white America. He opposed the concept of forced racial integration, using a personal example: "Milton Berle invited me to the hotel where he was performing and I went. But I wouldn't have gone there if I wasn't welcome." He deplored the fact that blacks trying to integrate were met with violence and concluded, "I'm not going to get killed trying to force myself on people who don't want me. I like my life." Finally, he complained that "people are always telling me what a good example I could set for my people if I just wasn't a Muslim." What he really wanted, he pleaded, "is peace—peace for myself and peace for the world" (Hauser 103).[17]

Here Ali answered those who criticized his racial views. Rather plaintively, he seemed to want to be left alone to fight and practice his faith, a wish that would never be granted given his growing fame as an important American icon.

Competing for attention with his religious views was talk of a rematch with Liston. Prior to the Miami fight, Ali's people had shaken hands with Liston's to seal a second fight in the unlikely event of an upset, with Liston's promoters paying Ali $50,000 for the right to promote the event. The bout would be set for Boston Garden in November 1964. Some U.S. senators, however, were suspicious of the circumstances in which the second fight was negotiated. Such rematch agreements were technically illegal, given the fact that they might cast suspicion that a champion could have a potential financial incentive to lose so as to pump an even bigger gate next time around. The Senate Antitrust and Monopoly sub-committee, however, found no evidence that Liston had thrown the first contest and thus did not try to prevent the fight.

In addition to attacks on his faith and questions about the rematch, Ali had to face a barrage of criticism involving his military draft status. In March 1962, Ali had been classified as 1-A (eligible to be drafted) by his selective service board in Louisville. When he went to take a prein-duction military qualifying examination in January 1964, shortly before the Liston fight, not surprisingly, he passed the physical component with ease. The mental aptitude test, however, utterly baffled him. He couldn't even figure out how many hours a person worked if he or she was on the job from 6:00 A.M. to 3:00 P.M. with an hour out for lunch. His Army IQ of 78 put him in the sixteenth percentile, far below minimum qualifica-tions for service. When he failed a second time in March 1964—under the supervision of three military psychiatrists to monitor the test—he was reclassified 1-Y (not qualified for service in the armed forces).

Ali poked fun at his low scores—"I said I was the greatest, not the smartest," he quipped to reporters (Bingham and Wallace 97). Congressional leaders were incensed, in part no doubt, because the reclas-sification came shortly after his public conversion to the Nation of Islam, and there was a great public outcry.[18] Representative William Ayers (R-Ohio) complained that "anybody who can throw a punch like Cassius ought to be able to throw a knife around a potato," and his Democratic colleague from South Carolina, Mendel Rivers, fumed during a speaking tour: "Clay's deferment is an insult to every mother's son serving in the armed forces" (Bingham and Wallace 97–98). A man from Idaho, writing to Secretary of the Army Stephen Ailes, "speculated that Ali had faked the results" (to which Ailes replied that is precisely the suspicion that led to his being retested). More ominously, a citizen wrote President Johnson that "unless Clay is drafted into the army, you will be *personally* sorry" (Italics in the original). Even more frighteningly, a lawyer from Georgia "started up a 'Draft That Nigger Clay' campaign" (Bingam and Wallace 101, 100, 97). The furor led Carl Vinson (D-Ga.), Chairman of the House Armed Services Committee, to demand an explanation from the Secretary of the Army. Ailes replied that the army would not alter its minimum standards merely because of "[Clay's] national prominence" (Hauser 143). The fuss soon died down temporarily, but even the media began to comment on Ali's intellectual limitations, using such language as "unsophisticated" and "lacking book learning" to describe the champion (Bingham and Wallace 99).

As this problem eased, other ones emerged. Before he began to train for his second match with Liston, Ali's faith would be both tested and enriched. Shortly after his victory over Liston, he became inadvertently embroiled in the growing dispute between Malcolm X and Elijah Muhammad. The two became increasingly alienated from each other. Malcolm embarked on a tour of Africa and the Middle East in the spring of 1964 and discovered to his satisfaction that Islam transcended race and that there were perfectly respectable and devout white Muslims. He shed his NOI name and adopted a more traditional Islamic one, El-Hajj Malik El-Shabbaz. Coincidentally, Ali made a pilgrimage to Africa that overlapped Malcolm's. But by May, when he left for Africa, Ali had clearly chosen to support Elijah in the great rift. Jim Brown recalls talking to Ali at some point after the Liston fight. The champion praised Elijah as a great man and confided to Brown that "he was going to have to reject Malcolm and choose Elijah." Ali himself indicated that he "believed Malcolm was wrong and Elijah's was God's messenger" (Hauser 110, 111).

The break was sealed when Malcolm happened to run into Ali in Accra, Ghana, as he was leaving for the airport. When he called out to his supposed close friend, "Brother Muhammad," Ali glanced at Malcolm and said coldly, "You left the Honorable Elijah Muhammad. That was the wrong thing to do." The two didn't even shake hands. As David Remnick notes, "It was a terrible moment for Malcolm.... [t] hrust out of the Nation of Islam..., he had been rejected in the harshest terms by Muhammad Ali, his great protégé and friend" (Remnick 215).[19]

Nonetheless, Ali found great solace in the Africa trip. He relished in the excitement of being in what he considered his homeland. He luxuriated in the honor of meeting such noted black African leaders as Ghana's liberator, Kwame Nkrumah. But most of all he enjoyed the common everyday Africans. His NOI friend Osman Karriem remembers that one day when they drove out of Accra, virtually no one could be seen. Then they heard drums beating, and soon people appeared lining the roads, screaming, "Ali! Ali!" Karriem was nonplussed as he looked over at Ali, wondering "what it must have been like for him to see thousands of people materialize out of nowhere and know they were there just for him." It was at that point, Karriem concluded, that "Cassius Clay came to an end and Muhammad Ali emerged" (Hauser 112).[20]

Ali experienced another major personal transformation that summer. Herbert Muhammad, one of Elijah's sons and Ali's chief minder, noticed that in Egypt his charge seemed to have quite a wandering eye as he more or less fell in love with every waitress he saw. When they returned to the United States, Herbert figured Ali needed to settle down and introduced him to Sonji Roi, a friend who worked the phones selling *Muhammad Speaks*. An extremely attractive young woman—and, interestingly, not a Muslim—she also worked as a cocktail waitress and had a reputation as a party girl. Ali was smitten immediately, and on their first date, on July 3, 1964, he asked her to marry him. Forty-one days later they were wed. In a later interview, Sonji said she agreed in part because she was lonely and could sense that Ali "needed a friend" (Hauser 115).[21]

With his personal life seemingly stabilized, Ali began to train for the Liston bout scheduled for November 16. But three days before the contest, Ali suffered an intestinal hernia that sent him to the hospital for surgery, canceling the rematch, which was rescheduled for May 25, 1965. He spent part of his recovery time doing some light training but was interrupted by news of the murder of Malcolm X. Ali's response was distant: "[He] was my friend… as long as he was a member of Islam." Ali denied that Elijah had anything to do with the shooting, saying, "We are not a violent people" (Remnick 240).

The champion and his entourage left for the Liston bout on April 1, arrived 50 hours later (the bus broke down en route), and then demanded the best suite at the best motel in Chiciopee Falls, Massachusetts, where he would finish his training. When told that someone was in it, Ali demanded, "Well get him out. The Greatest is here" (Remnick 243). But even the Greatest couldn't stand up to the Massachusetts Boxing Commission, which decided in early May not to sanction the fight, largely because of the suspected involvement of the mob.[22] Almost immediately, Mayor Robert T. Courturier from Lewiston, Maine, offered his small city as a replacement. Only 24 years old, the young mayor, perhaps naively, figured the fight would bring great positive publicity to his hometown.

There were problems almost immediately. The largest venue in the city was a hockey arena built for youth leagues, and there were only two undersized hotels and one night club, which featured the town's only stripper. More ominously, Ali's entourage now included several members of the NOI, "with their bow ties and steely theatrical stares" (Remnick 245).[23] There were rumors that hit men loyal to the slain Malcolm X were coming to assassinate Ali for disloyalty, while other rumors suggested that some of Elijah's followers had told Liston to lose or die. In the words of reporter Jerry Izenberg, "The atmosphere surrounding the fight was ugly" (Hauser 125).

On the night of the bout, the small arena wasn't even full, perhaps because the odds makers had made Sonny a 9–5 favorite, perhaps because prospective fans were afraid of the violence that rumor mongers predicted. The festivities got off to a rocky start when popular Broadway singing star Robert Goulet forgot the words to "The Star Spangled Banner." If anyone happened to be late either in Lewiston or in one of the many theaters where the fight was shown on closed-circuit television, they missed all the action. Ali knocked out the challenger less than two minutes into the fight. At the bell, Liston pressed Ali, trying to hit him with jabs. When one was slow and short, the champion caught the challenger with an overhand right to the temple. Liston immediately went down. In a bizarre chain of events, Ali refused to go to a neutral corner, standing over Liston, shouting, "Get up and fight, you bum. You're supposed to be so bad! Nobody will believe this" (Remnick 258). Later Ali admitted that he wanted Liston to recover so he could beat him even worse so he "could show everyone how great I was" (Hauser 128). The referee, former champion Jersey Joe Walcott, tried to push Ali back to his corner. Instead, the champ danced around the ring waving his hands in the air. Then, utter confusion: Ali went to his corner, but Walcott still didn't begin the count because he couldn't hear the knockdown counter at ringside. Screams of "Fix" roiled up from the small crowd. Liston stumbled to his feet, and Ali went after him. Nat Fleischer, editor of *Ring Magazine*, called Walcott over and told him to stop the fight because Liston had been on the canvas for 17 seconds. The official time keeper had stopped his count at 12. Walcott separated the two, and the fight officially ended.

Liston stumbled to his dressing room so groggy that he asked for smelling salts. In a touching moment, Floyd Patterson, whom Liston had knocked out twice in the 1st round in their previous championship fights, came to the dressing room and commiserated with the man who had destroyed him. Meanwhile, Ali, still in the ring, worried that Liston had taken a dive, but when he saw the instant replay, he was convinced that the blow was a lethal one: "The punch jarred him. It was a good punch" (Hauser 127). Later, he elaborated, claiming that the blow "was timed with rhythm and balance." Liston admitted that the punch had hurt him but claimed he stayed on the canvas so long because he thought Ali was "a nut" and would pound him if he tried to get up (Remnick 262).

Whatever history's final judgment on the punch, Ali retained his championship. At roughly the same time, President Lyndon Johnson and his advisors were debating whether to send additional U.S. combat troops to Vietnam. The president ordered just such an increase in late July, an action that would ultimately have a far more important impact on the life and career of Muhammad Ali than any argument over the nature of his knockout punch.[24]

NOTES

1. Liston worshiped Louis. He said after the second Patterson fight that Joe Louis was "the greatest champion of them all" and that he planned "to follow the example he set." Likewise, the Brown Bomber thought that Sonny was unstoppable: "Nobody's gonna beat Liston 'cept old age" (McRae 310).

2. Cannon's most famous and color-blind comment about Louis was that as a fighter and a person, Joe was "a credit to his race—the human race." Interestingly, Cannon was also highly critical of the color line in major league baseball. In a commentary on ABC Radio in 1945, he condemned America's pastime as "a game of prejudice, dominated by bigoted men with Jim Crow for an umpire" (McRae 239). ("Jim Crow" was the name given to the system of formal and informal racial segregation in the United States.)

3. Some observers disliked both fighters so intensely that they created some strange fantasies. Jim Murray, for example, speculated in the *Los Angeles Times* that "it would be the most popular fight since Hitler and Stalin—180,000,000 Americans rooting for a double knockout" (McRae 313).

4. Reporter Robert Lypsite was charmed by the meeting. Indeed, he saw Clay as a kind of fifth Beatle. In hindsight this was a momentous meeting between the music group and the athlete who were to become perhaps the most dominant world icons in popular culture in the 1960s. Of course, not all observers were so easily enthralled. The ever acerbic and increasingly conservative Jimmy Cannon thought they deserved each other because of the values they represented. They fit right in with "punks riding motorcycles with iron crosses,... college kids dancing naked,... and the surf bums who refuse to work" (Remnick 159). Clearly, a cultural chasm was beginning to yawn, one that would become increasingly obvious when Cassius Clay became Muhammad Ali and moved even further beyond the values of the Jimmy Cannons of the world.

5. Malcolm particularly appreciated Clay's kindness because Malcolm had recently been officially "silenced" by NOI leader Elijah Muhammad for 90 days (Relations between the two had been tense for several months). Malcolm was increasingly disillusioned because of rumors of Elijah's sexual dalliances with some of his female secretaries, while Elijah was angered by comments in which Malcolm seemed to approve of the assassination of John Kennedy. For the moment, Clay remained close to Malcolm while still revering Elijah.

6. It is interesting to compare Clay's behavior at the weigh-in with that of Joe Louis and Max Schmeling when they fought in 1936. The exchange on this occasion went:
Schmeling: "Hello, Joe. How do you do?"
Louis: "Fine, Max. And you?"

Schmeling: "Very good, Joe. Thank you…. Good luck this evening, Joe" (McRae 121).

Perhaps Schmeling was pulling a bit a reverse psychology, but the "confrontation" was certainly more decorous that the Clay–Liston imbroglio.

7. Liston's wife, Geraldine, confirmed that Clay's ploy was playing with her husband's head. In words eerily echoing Cassius's, she told Mort Sharnik just before the bout that Sonny thought Clay was "just out of his cotton-picking mind." She concluded that "you never know what to expect from a man like that,… a madman" (Remnick 182).

8. According to Jose Torres, Clay said, "I've got you now, *chump*," an epithet that seems more in line with Clay's usual patter directed at the champ (Torres 136).

9. Cassius admits that Liston did catch him with a left hook, but he obviously survived; a major confidence builder (Hauser 75).

10. David Remnick believes the story, saying that it was "as close to reliable as it gets in boxing." According to McKinney, Pollino told him that such a back-up plan was standard operating procedure in the Liston camp (Remnick 195). Dundee insisted that it was an accident, although the commercial film, *Ali*, repeated McKinney's version. As a sidebar, Dundee recalls that two men from the NOI who were near Cassius's corner looked at him as if he had sabotaged Clay's chances.

11. Remnick claims that Cassius "assumed that… everyone knew that he was a convert" to the NOI. However, this seems unlikely, given Clay's efforts at keeping his visits to mosques a secret.

12. Muhammad, of course, was the great Prophet and founder of Islam, and Ali was his cousin and founder of the Shia branch of Islam. Muhammad means "one worthy of praise" (Remnick 213).

13. In fact, Dundee claimed that he thought Muslim was a kind of cloth (Remnick 209).

14. Liberal Republican Senator Jacob Javits from New York also supported Ali's right to choose his religious faith, although he distanced himself from Russell's view of civil rights. Historian Jeffrey Sammons rightly points out that the fact that Ali's name and religion were being discussed on the floor of the U.S. Senate "was clear proof that the heavyweight title was an instrument of symbolic power beyond the sport" (Sammons 196).

15. According to an FBI log from a wiretap on King's telephone, the civil rights activist eventually phoned Clay, who told King that he was his "brother" and that he was "with him 100 [percent]" but that he "couldn't take any chances" by publicly supporting King. He concluded by warning King to "watch out for them whites," not bad advice considering the FBI's activities in regard to King (Remnick 211). The FBI, incidentally, consistently referred to Ali as Clay.

16. Not all observers, however, condemned Ali for his religious faith. Writing in the *Chicago Defender* a month after the fight, black baseball legend Jackie Robinson praised Ali's skill and pooh poohed the influence of the Muslims: "I

don't think Negroes en masse will embrace Black Muslimism," he wrote. If they ever did, the commitment would not be the result of Ali's influence but rather "because white America had. . . . refused to grant us the same rights that any other citizen enjoys in this land" (Remnick 212).

17. Milton Berle was a leading comedian in the 1950s and early 1960s.

18. There was a less public outcry as well. According to Ali's good friend Howard Bingham, the day after Ali announced that he had converted to the NOI, J. Edgar Hoover, director of the FBI, "ordered agents to inquire about the boxer's draft status. The easiest way to keep a troublemaker in line, he figured, would be to keep him under the watchful eye of Uncle Sam for two years" (Bingham and Wallace 96). When Ali was later reclassified, Hoover was convinced that he had failed intentionally and had agents check Ali's high school record. The fact that Cassius barely earned a certificate of attendance and scored 83 on an IQ test administered by the Army seemed to validate its decision.

19. In his most recent memoir, Ali expresses profound sadness for this act of betrayal: "Turning my back on Malcolm was one of the mistakes that I regret most in my life. I wish I had been able to tell Malcolm I was sorry, that he was right about so many things." Without Malcolm, Ali admits, "I might never have become a Muslim" (Ali, *Butterfly* 85).

20. David Remnick went further, suggesting that the visit to Africa showed that Ali had become "an international symbol, a fighter bigger than the heavyweight champion, the most famous person in the world" (Remnick 214).

21. Sonji continued to call herself Sonji Clay after they were divorced in early 1966.

22. Such involvement was never proved. Perhaps the commission was simply worried about Ali's religious conversion and the forbidding atmosphere created by the Muslims who had joined his retinue.

23. Even Angelo Dundee became nervous. When he touched the arm of one of the Muslim women in camp while thanking her for doing some sewing for him, a Muslim bodyguard pulled him aside and castigated him: "Don't you ever put your hand on one of the sisters again" (Remnick 245).

24. The debate about the second Ali–Liston fight has continued. Initially, a number of reporters such as Gene Ward of the *New York Daily News* believed there was something fishy about the punch. Jose Torres thought that Liston failed to get up because Ali had "psyched [him] out" and because he "feared the Black Muslims" (Torres 154). The FBI briefly investigated unsubstantiated claims that Liston had told his wife he was going to throw the fight—a charge Geraldine Liston denied—but decided not to pursue the issue. Liston himself years later told reporter Jerry Izenberg that he lost for one simple reason: Nat Fleischer "could count to ten faster that Joe Walcott" (Remnick 266).

Cassius Clay (center) strolls around the Olympic Village in Rome in 1960, showing off his Gold Medal with other American boxing champions, Wilbert McClure (l) and Edward Crook. (AP/Wide World Photos)

Muhammad Ali (standing, far left) cranes his neck to see his religious idol and mentor, Nation of Islam leader Elijah Muhammad (at podium). (Photofest)

ABC sports commentator and friend Howard Cosell (with mic on left) interviews Muhammad Ali at the armed services induction center in Houston. On April 28, 1967, Ali refused to be inducted into the military and was soon stripped of his title. (AP/Wide World Photos)

Ali employs his "rope-a-dope" strategy against George Foreman. Ali won a stunning upset victory, regaining the heavyweight championship on October 30, 1974. (AP/Wide World Photos)

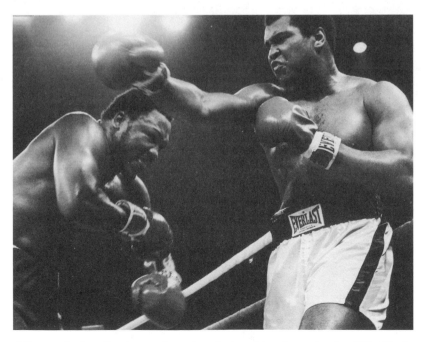

Ali pounds Joe Frazier, as he wins their rubber bout in the "Thrilla in Manilla" on October 1, 1975. (Photofest)

Ali married his third wife, Veronica Porsche, in 1977. They were divorced nine years later. (Photofest)

Ali lights his torch from the one carried by U.S. swimming champion, Janet Evans. He then completed the final leg in the torch lighting ceremony at the 1996 Olympics in Atlanta. (AP/Wide World Photos)

Chapter 5

THE BRIEF ASCENDANCY AND LONG FALL: JUNE 1965–APRIL 1967

Ali's defense of his title against Liston silenced most of his boxing critics, despite some lingering doubts about Liston's rapid exit. Clearly, the young champion was a superior fighter, which became a major problem for Ali and for the heavyweight division. Put simply, there were no legitimate contenders on the horizon. No one seemed to want a third Liston bout, and the two most obvious contenders, Cleveland Williams and Eddie Machen, had previously suffered knockouts at the hands of Liston. Ali, only half kidding, encouraged the search for a "Great White Hope" to challenge him, because he assumed that a strong Caucasian opponent would "jack up the purse as no black opponent could" (Remnick 271). And so with no viable challenges, Ali went on world tour for the rest of the summer, fighting exhibitions in places such as Puerto Rico, Sweden, London, and Belize.

Ali no doubt needed the distraction. Relations with his wife, Sonji, had reached a breaking point. His Muslim advisors were increasingly concerned about his non-Muslim wife's failure to adhere to Islamic rules and practices. In essence, they told him to choose between Sonji and his faith. He made his choice on June 23, 1965, when he petitioned the Dade County, Florida, circuit court to annul the marriage. His testimony focused on Sonji's failure to abide by the Muslim dress code. He complained especially about an outfit she wore during a press conference prior to the second Liston bout: "You could see all of her! The seams of her underwear! Tight pants around all those men was wrong" (Remnick 267). The proceedings dragged on until January 1966 when a divorce was finally granted.[1]

Ali returned from his exhibition tour with a new purpose—to fight and defeat former champion Floyd Patterson. Ever since Ali's official conversion to the Nation of Islam, Patterson had been attacking him. In an article in *Sports Illustrated* in October 1964, Patterson condemned the NOI because it denied the integrationist vision that he trumpeted. True brotherhood "will never come about if we think the way the Black Muslims think." In fact, "Clay" had done enormous damage by joining a religion that preached "hate and separation instead of love and integration." Snorted Patterson, "He might as well have joined the Ku Klux Klan" (Remnick 273). Patterson saw himself as a kind, great, true black hope who would do what Sonny Liston didn't have the courage to do: defeat a man who was leading African Americans astray. Patterson kept up the drumbeat in another article in *Sports Illustrated* a few weeks before his bout with Ali, scheduled for November 1965. He said flatly that "the image of a Black Muslim as the world heavyweight champion disgraces the sport and the nation." Patterson promised to be the agent who would make sure that "the Black Muslims' scourge [is] removed from boxing" (Remnick 275).

Ali did not take kindly to such an attack. Even before the second Liston fight, he managed to razz Patterson, who was training for his next bout. Ali showed up at his training camp "with an armful of lettuce and carrots, shouting that he wanted nothing more that to drive 'the rabbit' back into his hole." He then called Patterson "an Uncle Tom Negro, a white man's Negro" and offered to fight him "then and there" (Remnick 272). To be sure, Ali often raided his opponents' camps, taunting with an undertone of humor. But with Patterson, he was much more serious. Ali increased the severity of verbal jabs before their bout. He attacked Patterson for moving into an all-white neighborhood and claimed that "the only time he'd be caught in Harlem was when he was in the back of a car in some parade" (Hauser 139). As the fight with Patterson neared, he further raised the level of vitriol. Reacting to Patterson's claim that he was going to "bring the title back to America," Ali responded, "I'm American. But he's [Patterson] a deaf dumb so-called Negro who needs a spanking" (Hauser 140). And this time when he resorted to verse, it was filled with spite and anger:

I'm going to put him flat on his back,
So that he will start acting black (Cottrell 238).

Finally, Ali shot back: "Why should I let an old Negro make a fool out of me" (Remnick 278).

Five days before the fight, Ali made a pilgrimage from Las Vegas to Phoenix, Arizona, to receive spiritual counsel from Elijah Mohammad, who was there on a rest cure. When he returned to Vegas, according to biographer John Cottrell, he was "in a gay, light hearted mood," seemingly over his anger. At the weigh-in, in marked contrast to the one at the first Liston bout, Ali was remarkably subdued. Nonetheless Cottrell concluded that Ali's overall behavior before the fight "can only be described as unnecessarily spiteful" (Cottrell 240, 239).[2] As for Patterson, rumors flew that he was preparing for another quick and anonymous get away after the bout, as he had with Liston. A number of his training sessions were held without the press admitted, and in general, an element of gloom hung over the Patterson camp. The main positive event for Patterson prior to the bout was the support of singer Frank Sinatra. The famed crooner fully backed the challenger and invited him to his suite at the Sands Hotel on the morning of the bout. According to Patterson, Sinatra said that "many people in America"—including Frank himself—"were counting on me to win back the championship from Clay" (Remnick 279).

A torrential rainstorm on the night of the fight kept the crowd to a rather meager 8,000 (although many more watched on closed-circuit television). In an unusual interview held just prior to entering the ring, Ali revealed his strategy. He "would not go for a knock out." Rather he would "punish Patterson so much that detectives should be detailed to follow him for the next three days to make sure that he does nothing wrong" (Cottrell 243). Muhammad Ali was still coldly furious, and in what most observers saw as a tasteless, horrific exhibition, Ali humiliated Floyd Patterson.

The fight was indeed a travesty. According to David Remnick, "The first round was the worst of all" (Remnick 280). The champion simply flitted around the lunging Patterson, barely deigning to flick an occasional jab and easily avoiding Patterson's futile punches. Most humiliating to Patterson, Ali taunted as he danced: "Come on American. Come on white American." At the end of the round, according to John Cottrell, his "final act of insolence was to turn swiftly on his heels... and stride truculently back to his corner" (Cottrell 243). For the next 11 rounds, Ali alternately pummeled Patterson and teased him, refusing to deliver the knock-out blow of which everyone in the arena knew he was capable. In the middle of the 2nd round, Ali had the gall to allow Patterson to rest on one knee while he jauntily strode around the ring. Throughout the fight, Ali continued his taunting, urging Patterson to try harder, while during clinches the champion kept up the racial patter: "Uncle Tom, Uncle Tom, white man's nigger" (Remnick 281).

The crowd spent much of the bout jeering at Ali. Even Angelo Dundee urged the champ to finish the job. When referee Harry Krause tried to stop the fight after the 11th round, Patterson refused to let him. Somehow, he must have thought that there was still a chance for him break his own record and wear the heavyweight championship belt for an unprecedented third time. But in the 12th round, Krause saw that if he allowed the fight to continue, the pathetic Patterson might suffer permanent damage. In spite of Patterson's protests, he ended the torture.[3]

After the fight, Patterson went to Frank Sinatra's suite to apologize for losing and letting down the great American pop icon. As he remembers it, Sinatra listened briefly, then snubbed the defeated fighter by walking away from him. Patterson "got the message [and] left" (Remnick 283). But apparently he didn't get the message about Ali's utter superiority as a fighter. Later Patterson actually fantasized that when Ali was drafted into the military, Patterson might volunteer for the service himself: "They have boxing matches [in the army]. Maybe I could fight Clay in one and beat him and regain my title" (Cottrell 246–47).

As for Ali, after the fight he claimed to reporters that Patterson had taken "his best punches" and that he would have knocked out the challenger if he could have. He said that he had to retreat several times to rest because he was tiring. Ali left the Las Vegas Convention Hall, surrounded by members of the NOI and three Muslim women from Pakistan, for a victory party at the Sands Hotel. Ali, who claimed that his right hand was badly hurt, shook hands with his left. His estranged wife, Sonji, and estranged friend, Bundini Brown, comforted each other on the edges of the party.

Two of Ali's heroes—Sugar Ray Robinson and Jackie Robinson—also were estranged from him during the period surrounding the Patterson bout. Whenever he saw Sugar Ray, Ali would say, "The king, the master, my idol!" (McRae 330). And he clearly wanted Sugar Ray to join his camp before the Patterson fight. But the NOI complications were insurmountable. Jackie likewise distanced himself, this time over what he saw as "Clay's viciousness" in the ring. The champion had "played and toyed" with Patterson, "torturing him with an unforgivable cruelty" (McRae 330).[4]

Most observers of boxing also didn't buy Ali's lament that he had really tried to finish off Patterson. They agreed that the bout was a travesty. Robert Lipsyte of the *New York Times*, long one of Ali's major journalistic supporters, said that Ali's tactics reminded him of "a little boy pulling off the wings of a butterfly piecemeal," while a headline in *Life Magazine* referred to the "Sickening Spectacle in the Ring." Yet Lipsyte also conceded "Ali's incomparable artistry in the ring." Sportswriter Gil Rogin captured the paradox: "What a strange, uncommon man is Clay. Who can fathom him? We can only watch him... and ponder whether, despite his often truly affecting ways, he doesn't scorn us and the world he is champion of" (Hauser 141).[5]

During the year and a half after the Patterson fight, Ali's life moved on two very different tracks—the professional and the personal. In the ring, he successfully defended his championship seven times, although not always convincingly. But outside the ring, he experienced a set of unsettling circumstances—from his divorce from Sonji to a barrage of criticism over his decision to refuse military induction. These blows might well have destroyed a lesser man.

As might be expected, the two lives often intersected, most prominently around Ali's status in the military draft. During 1965, President Johnson escalated the Vietnam war far beyond what Presidents Eisenhower and Kennedy had envisioned. Johnson continued to pour money, military equipment, and U.S. military advisors into South Vietnam to keep it from falling to communist forces. But when this effort did not stem the tide, in rapid order, he authorized the sustained bombing of communist North Vietnam, introduced American combat Marines to guard air bases in the South, and soon changed their mission to offensive ground action against communist forces in South Vietnam. This escalation meant that draft calls would need to be raised in the future. Thus, in early 1966, the Pentagon lowered the percentile rating required on the mental aptitude test from the 30th to the 15th percentile. (Ali had ranked between the 16th and 18th in his previous tests.) When the head of the Selective Service system in Kentucky announced that Ali would soon be drafted, the fighter's lawyer, Edward Jacko, went before Ali's Louisville draft board on February 14, 1966, and petitioned it to defer the young fighter on a number of grounds, including financial hardship. But on February 17, the board declared Cassius Clay eligible for the draft.[6]

Ali was in Miami when he heard the decision. Robert Lipsyte also happened to be in town and was actually visiting with the champ when he found out. Ali was staying in a rented house in a black neighborhood. When Lipsyte arrived on the lawn, he saw the champion "watch the girls walk by. They'd slow down when they saw him, and from time to time he'd sing, 'Hey little girl in the high school sweater'" (Hauser 144). This innocent flirting came to a halt when a local reporter called to inform Ali that his draft status had been changed to I-A. His first reaction was intensely personal and even selfish. According to Lipsyte, he simply exclaimed, "How can they do this to me? I don't want my career ruined"

(Hauser 144). Then his Muslim friends and body guards began to politicize the issue: "This is how the White Devils do you.... Some fat cracker sergeant's going to drop a hand grenade down your pants" (Bingham and Wallace 113–14). As Ali became increasingly upset, the phone started ringing off the hook as various news agencies pestered him for a response to the draft board's action. Most of the questions had to do with Ali's attitude toward the war in Vietnam. When asked where the country was located, he responded, "Well, it's out there somewhere. I don't know." Some enterprising caller even asked him about his view of the Gulf of Tonkin Resolution. When one caller inquired what he thought of the Viet Cong, Ali yelled in frustration, "Man, I ain't got no quarrel with them Viet Cong" (Hauser 145). This quotation became one of the most famous in the Ali lexicon. As John Condon, head of publicity at Madison Square Garden, put it, the statement gave his enemies the opportunity to "[make] him an unpatriotic draft dodger" (Hauser 145).[7]

The public outrage was predictable. Sportswriters were almost unanimous in their condemnations. To Red Smith, "Cassius [made] himself as sorry a spectacle as those unwashed punks who picket and demonstrate against the war." If Smith compared Ali to hated antiwar demonstrators, Milton Gross contrasted him to the "the kids slogging through the rice paddies" of Vietnam. Journalist Murray Robinson reminded his readers that "Clay" was an "adult brat, who had boasted ad nauseam about his fighting skill." To Robinson, the Viet Cong comment, however, was beyond the pale. He had "squealed like a cornered rat when tapped for the army" and "should be shorn of his title" (Hauser 145). Jim Murray of the *Los Angeles Times* put it succinctly when he called Ali a "black Benedict Arnold" (Bingham and Wallace 120).

According to Howard Bingham, the night after Ali's remark appeared in the media, his telephone rang constantly, and anonymous threats poured in. Echoing Murray Robinson, one caller exclaimed, "You cowardly, turncoat black rat.... If I had a bomb, I'd blow you to hell," while another—a woman—asked venomously, "You better'n than my son?" She spat out the answer to her own rhetorical question: "You black bastard. I pray to God they draft you tomorrow. Draft you and shoot you on the spot" (Ali, *The Greatest* 124).

Former prize fighters joined the chorus of dissent. Former heavyweight contender Billy Conn said indignantly, "I'll never go to another one of his fights. He is a disgrace to the boxing profession" (Hauser 147). Former champion Gene Tunney wrote to Ali: "You have disgraced your title and the American flag. Apologize for your remarks or you will be barred from the ring." Jack Dempsey, from whom Tunney had wrested the title, spoke more ominously: "Muhammad Ali is finished.… . He should be careful. It's not safe for him to be on the streets" (Bingham and Wallace 121, 120).

But Ali remembers that he also began to receive a few quiet calls of support in the days that followed his Viet Cong comment, especially from antiwar students wanting him to speak on their campuses. Most memorable was a call from Bertrand Russell, the noted British philosopher and antiwar activist (although Ali admitted that he had never heard of him). Russell thanked Ali for his statement about the Viet Cong. Ali claimed to be an athlete, not a political thinker, then asked Russell whom he would pick in a bout between him and British challenger Henry Cooper. When Russell picked Ali, the champ invited him ringside if a London bout with Cooper was ever finalized. The philosopher later sent Ali a letter, warning him that the U.S. government and other of his enemies "will try to break you because you are a symbol of a force they are unable to destroy,… a whole people determined no longer to be butchered and debased with fear and oppression" (Remnick 288).[8]

But Bertrand Russell hardly represented mainstream opinion, at least in the United States where it counted. In the United States, boxing officials—a far more crucial group than Russell and his fellow opponents of the war—were deeply disturbed by Ali's comments. Here, the personal and professional did intersect with increasingly ominous consequences for Ali. His next scheduled fight was in Chicago on March 29, 1966, against Windy City native Ernie Terrell, who also held the heavyweight championship that was sanctioned by the World Boxing Association. Because of Terrell's popularity in his home town, the fact that it also housed the headquarters of the Nation of Islam, and the prospect of unifying the title, the bout looked to be a tremendous financial success. But newspapers in Chicago and soon all over the United States called on the Illinois State Athletic Commission to rescind the license for the fight. Ali refused to apologize to the Commission for his comments about Vietnam, but before the Commission could act, in late February, Illinois Attorney General William Clark declared the license illegal and cancelled the bout.[9] The two camps scrambled to find another venue, but every U.S. city they approached bowed to public pressure and refused to sanction the fight. Even Louisville, Ali's hometown, rejected its native son after the Kentucky State Senate passed a resolution condemning the champion for "[bringing] discredit to all loyal Kentuckians and to the names of the thousands who gave their lives for this country during his lifetime" (Hauser 147).

Canadians, however, many of whom actively opposed the Vietnam War, seemed to have no such patriotic qualms about Ali's stand on the

Viet Cong. Maple Leaf Gardens in Toronto agreed to host the bout, but Terrell backed out. Because a number of American theaters refused to show the fight on closed circuit, the financial rewards Terrell hoped for had seriously diminished. Ali's handlers managed to convince Canadian heavyweight champion, George Chuvalo, to step in a month before the bout, which unleashed another storm of criticism in the United States. Arthur Daley of the *New York Times* rehashed all the old charges against Ali—his boasting, his connection to the Nation of Islam, and "his disdain for the decency of even a low-grade patriotism." He urged that the bout be boycotted as a way of "showing [American] resentment at a production that thumbs its nose at the public." Congressman Frank Clark (D-Pa.) took to the floor of the House of Representatives and simply stated that "the heavyweight champion turns my stomach" (Hauser 147). Clark, like Daley, urged that all citizens of the United States boycott the fight.

Such pleas, however, did nothing to deter Ali and Chuvalo.[10] Ali launched his usual sportive verbal assault on the challenger. He called the Canadian "the washerwoman" and complained that the bout would be too easy: "A den of rattlesnakes couldn't shake me," he boasted, because Allah would surely protect him. Chuvalo countered with the claim that he was rougher than Ali, especially "in close" where he would be "the boss" (Hauser 149). The boss was no match for the champion, however, although the fight did last the full 15 rounds. But Chuvalo took the majority of the punishment, winning at most only one of the rounds.[11] As Chuvalo put it in an interview with Thomas Hauser, he thought he had at least done a little damage, especially with body blows: "They said he [Ali] was peeing blood after the fight." But in the end, according to the Canadian, Ali was "just so damn fast" (Hauser 149).

On the draft front, even before the Chuvalo fight, Ali's lawyers continued to try to find a legal way for their client to avoid conscription. He appeared before his local selective service board on March 17, 1966, arguing again that he and his parents would suffer great financial distress were he to be drafted. But he also appealed for conscientious objector (CO) status based on his Islamic beliefs. The draft board denied the request, and affirmed its denial in May 1966.

In the meantime, the champion at least temporarily escaped the hullabaloo surrounding his draft status by scheduling three title defenses in Europe between May and September 1966. The trip helped Ali "regain his old spirit," at least temporarily (Bingham and Wallace 133). He also solidified his growing friendship with sportscaster Howard Cosell, who was broadcasting the bout.[12] Ali even began writing prebout poetry again. Prior to his May 21 rematch with British heavyweight Henry Cooper, he composed a mini-epic that combined a somewhat playful attack on his critics with the usual braggadocio about his athletic prowess. Ali wrote, "I won't let critics seal my fate" and concluded that he was "still the greatest" (Bingham and Wallace 134).

Henry Cooper certainly would agree with the last line of this ditty. Ali battered him for six rounds, inflicting what British promoter Mickey Duff called "one of the worst cuts I've ever seen" over Cooper's left eye (Hauser 153). Then on August 6, Ali defended his title, again in London, knocking out Britisher Brian London in three rounds.[13]

Shortly after this fight, on August 17, Ali's out of the ring problems once again dominated his life. He appeared before a special meeting of the Kentucky Selective Service Appeal Board to petition to have his local draft board's decision to draft him overturned. The NOI had also hired a new lawyer to assist in the case. Hayden Covington Jr., who had defended Jehovah's Witnesses during World War II, believed that Ali's attorneys had erred in focusing primarily on the CO issue. Even if given this status, he would still have to serve in a noncombat role—something that he did not want to do. Thus Covington moved to add to the grounds for the appeal that Ali was a Muslim minister, and all ministers were exempt from service. Ali had spent the previous two years occasionally preaching in NOI mosques. In a letter to the hearing officer, retired Kentucky circuit court judge Lawrence Grauman, Ali asserted that "the Holy Qur'an ... [tells us] that we are not to participate in wars on the side of non-believers." Thus, his religious faith would not allow him "even as much aid [in a war] as passing a cup of water to the wounded" (Hauser 155). At the hearing, Ali added that "90 percent of his time was devoted to preaching and converting people" (Bingham and Wallace 130). Although Grauman did not buy the exemption argument, in a decision that no doubt stunned everyone associated with the case, he recommended that the conscientious objector claim be upheld. He said that Ali was "of good character, morals, and integrity, and sincere in his objection [to the war] on religious grounds" (Hauser 155). The U.S. Justice Department argued that the recommendation should be ignored. According to T. Oscar Smith, Chief of the Department's Conscientious Objector Section, because Ali had not used religious reasons at his first hearing in February 1966, his beliefs must be "a matter of convenience and not sincerely held" (Bingham and Wallace 131).[14] The Kentucky Appeal Board sided with the federal government's view, ignored Grauman's recommendation, and denied the CO request.[15]

After another defense of his title on September 10, 1966, this time a 12th round knockout of German heavyweight Karl Mildenberger, Ali made a business decision that would further anger many white Americans. When his five-year contract with the Louisville Sporting Group ran out, Herbert Muhammad became his new general manager, and Angelo Dundee was retained at chief ring manager. Herbert made out quite well financially, getting a 40 percent cut of Ali's income-generating activity (later raised by Ali himself to two-thirds of the total take). According to Elijah Muhammad, the NOI took this unusual step even though he knew boxing was "a crooked business." He claimed that "we want Muhammad [Ali] to get justice out of it" (Hauser 156).

The new management team quickly arranged a title defense against Cleveland Williams. Probably because Ali's draft problems seemed to be at least temporarily settled when his appeal was turned down, the Texas State Boxing Commission allowed the fight to be held in Houston at the Astrodome. Williams had been a feared puncher in the early 1960s, but a confrontation with a Texas patrolman led to his being shot in the colon. Four operations later, he was not much of a challenge, although his manager put up a brave front. He claimed that "Cleve... crushes bones with either hand" but would be an exemplary champion because he "goes to church on Sunday, don't drink, and is married to a preacher's daughter." That would be a Christian church and daughter, of course (Hauser 159). For his part, Ali calmly announced to reporters that he would introduce a new wrinkle during the bout: the "Ali shuffle... , a step he promised would sweep the nation as the hottest dance innovation since the twist" (Hauser 159). Out of the public eye, however, Ali was more sensitive to the fact that Williams was hardly the fighter he had been before he had been shot. He privately told Jerry Izenberg that he was bothered by the fact that Williams had little of his ability left. The reporter replied, "If you want to do this guy a favor, knock him out as soon as you can." Izenberg was afraid that Williams might really suffer permanent damage if the fight lasted too long (Hauser 160).

Ali may well have taken pity on Williams because of his condition. The fight was brutal and quick, and Ali knocked out the challenger in the 3rd round before 35, 450 fans—the largest crowd ever to witness an indoor boxing match up to that time. Williams must have realized that he had no chance, even though he was only a 5–1 underdog. Prior to the fight, Williams initially refused to come out of the dressing room and enter the ring until promoter Bob Arum told him if he didn't fight he wouldn't received any proceeds from the bout.

Howard Cosell thought that this was Ali's greatest pugilistic performance: "That night he was the most devastating fighter who ever lived. He dominated from the opening." By the 3rd round, Williams had gone down four times and was gushing blood from the mouth. According to Cosell, Williams had barely touched Ali, who was faster and bigger, "bold and young and strong and skilled, just coming into his prime as a fighter" (Hauser 160).

Three months after pummeling Williams, Ali returned to the Astrodome to finally face Ernie Terrell in the bout that had been cancelled the previous year in Chicago. Perhaps the lure of a big crowd and the relative quiescence of the draft issue convinced the Texas Boxing Commission to approve another Ali fight. Interestingly, Terrell was the World Boxing Association (WBA) champion, while Ali was recognized as champion by the most powerful state commissions in places such as New York, Pennsylvania, and Texas. The WBA (which had stripped Ali of the title in 1964) allowed Terrell to put it on the line, a further inducement for Ali.

The two fighters had actually known each other for several years prior to their February fight. They had been on the same card in a match in Miami in 1962; Terrell was planning to fly back to Chicago, but Ali offered to take him in his red Cadillac as far as Louisville. Terrell remembers that they stopped at an all-black college in Chattanooga, where students were cool toward to Ali. They didn't respond positively to his standard NOI drill about a Canadian coming from Canada but there is no country called "Negro." One student quipped with a certain degree of logic that he had "never heard of a country called 'white folks' either" (Hauser 162–63). Ali left in a huff but did allow Terrell to spend the night at his parents' home before Terrell caught a bus the next day.

If there had been a budding friendship, it didn't survive the prefight hoopla. According to Terrell, the promoter wanted the two opponents to come to Houston two weeks before the bout in order to ballyhoo it and build the crowd. Terrell remembers saying, "It's alright with me if it's alright with Clay." Terrell's use of "Clay" angered and upset Ali: "Why can't you call me Muhammad Ali? You're just an Uncle Tom" (Hauser 163). Terrell claimed he didn't mean to provoke; he just remembered Ali as Clay, in part because of the car trip to Louisville. But once Ali got as angry as he did, Terrell decided to keep using the "slave name," figuring it would help build the gate. He assumed Ali wouldn't mind. He was wrong; Ali was livid. It looked like it would be the Floyd Patterson brouhaha revisited.

The fight itself, however, was very different from the Patterson match. Although angry at Patterson, Ali mainly toyed with the former champ, inflicting pain but never really trying to hurt him seriously, just keeping him around to beat up on. With Terrell, Ali displayed a level of viciousness and sheer brutality absent from the Patterson bout. Early on, a series of blows to the face caused a bone to fracture under the challenger's left eye. Terrell claimed that Ali exacerbated the wound illegally by thumbing the eye after rubbing his glove against the rope to shred it. Ali claims that this never happened.[16] Whatever the truth, there is no doubt that Ali's anger overwhelmed him. After the 8th round, Terrell was helpless, and Ali clearly wanted to keep him around to punish. The champion kept yelling, "What's my name?" and then attacked Terrell's injured eye (Remnick 289). By the final round, Terrell mainly stumbled around in a crouch, almost like a frightened bug. Ali never knocked him out.

The public reaction was immediate and negative. Any good will Ali built up after the Williams fight dissipated as the press savaged the champion just as Ali had brutalized Terrell. Most writers focused on the cruelty. In the *New York Daily News*, Gene Ward called the fight "a disgusting exhibition of calculating cruelty," while Milton Gross said that Ali "had turned people's stomachs" (Hauser 165). Jimmy Cannon widened the net, seeing Ali as a truly "perverse" person who claimed to be a minister while handing out such punishment. Cannon also revisited the old charge that by being a Muslim, Ali was actually supporting the Ku Klux Klan (Remnick 289). Even friends such as reporter Jerry Izenberg said that in the bout, Muhammad Ali was simply "evil" (Hauser 164).

But the most chilling comment came from a member of the public even before the fight had begun. As Ali entered the Astrodome, he recognized a striking white woman who had also been at the Cleveland Williams bout. (Ali had nicknamed her Miss Velvet Green because of the color of her dress.) She pushed her way into the entourage, asking for an autograph, and told Ali, "I come to all your fights." When the champion signed her notepad, thanked her, and said he wanted her to continue, she replied, "I will... until I see them take you out on a stretcher." Raising her voice she continued, "God won't always let evil win.... I'm going to be there when they bust your face and stomp it in." It was, Ali admits, his most vivid memory of that night (Ali, *Greatest* 163).[17]

Ali said he had trouble understanding all the fuss about the alleged brutality of the fight. Why should he be criticized for doing what he was supposed to do: "It's just a job," he pointed out. "Grass grows, birds fly, waves pound the sand, I beat people up" (Bingham and Wallace 138). Such a stand was, of course, naïve. If Ali was to convince the Selective Service that he was a conscientious objector because of his status as a Muslim minister, such seemingly vindictive violence as he displayed against Terrell could only hurt his case.

The Nation of Islam continued to help its most famous adherent in his appeal to the government. Its official publication, *Muhammad Speaks*, blared in banner headlines on March 3: "World Champion Moves Closer to Full-Time Task as Muhammad's Minister." The story noted that Ali had moved to Houston in order to "take complete charge" of that city's mosque while its usual minister was on a "leave of absence." The story concluded that reaction among blacks in Houston, both Muslim and non-Muslim was "highly favorable" (Bingham and Wallace 138).

The National Selective Service Presidential Appeal Board did not buy this argument and rejected Ali's final appeal on March 6, 1967. His lawyers did convince the government to move the date of induction from April 11 (in Louisville) to April 28 (in Houston). Ali's legal team also really thought that the end of the line had come, that Ali might actually wind up in jail.[18] Ali, meanwhile, both continued to express his opposition to the war and prepared for what would be his last fight until he fought again in October 1970. Playing the race card, he became more firm in his opposition to the war, telling Sports Illustrated, for example, that he did not want to "put on a uniform and... drop bombs... on brown people in Vietnam while so-called Negro people in Louisville are treated like dogs." Even the prospect of jail seemed not to deter him, and he said, almost stoically, "I have nothing to lose by following my beliefs. We've [African Americans] been in jail for four hundred years" (Remnick 289, 290). Of course, he continued to be hammered by many in the general public. Ali was in Chicago on the day he got his notice. While walking quietly down the street, he was accosted by a group of drunken American Legionnaires, one of whom exclaimed, "They gotcha! Son of a bitch. Thank God they gotcha" (Bingham and Wallace 139).

The fight against journeyman Zora Folley on March 22, 1967, seemed almost an afterthought. It was noteworthy because it was the first heavyweight championship in 16 years held at New York City's Madison Square Garden. To increase the size of the crowd, Garden officials even alluded to Ali's draft woes on the auditorium marquee that announced the bout. In a poetic ditty, the marquee displayed: "Last Chance to See Ali/Before He Gets One to Three" (a reference to the normal jail sentence for refusing military induction). There was also the usual public outcry that he would dare to fight under the circumstances. Congressman Robert Michel (R-IL), for example, condemned "the illustrious Cassius Clay" on the House floor "for scheduling another alleged bout to milk a few more dollars out of dodging the draft." He concluded, in horror, that "apparently Cassius will fight anybody but the Vietcong" (Bingham and Wallace 139–40).

Ali easily disposed of Folley, knocking him out in the 7th round. The challenger praised Ali's skills, claiming that he was so good that the legends of the past—Dempsey, Tunney, even Louis and Marciano—could not have stayed with him. "He could write the book on boxing," Folley concluded (Hauser 167). As it turned out, it would be a book that Muhammad Ali would have plenty of time to compose.

Ali's lawyers had one last card to play before he was to be inducted into the military. They had secured a hearing in the Federal District Court in Houston to seek a restraining order against the Selective Service so that the agency could not say that Ali was delinquent if he refused to be inducted. This would at least give his legal team more time to mount additional appeals in civil court. Ali was spending some time in Chicago after the Folley bout, and he flew to Houston on April 27. During the flight, the captain of the plane announced that Ali was on board. When the aircraft met some unexpected heavy turbulence—dishes were careening throughout the cabin—the champ noticed a panicked woman across the aisle. According to Howard Bingham, she "had a Bible and was praying out loud. As her eyes met Ali's, she pointed a finger and started screaming at him, 'God is punishing us because he [Clay] is on the plane. He's punishing us because we're helping His enemy'" (Bingham and Wallace 146). Apparently God had second thoughts, because the plane landed safely, and Ali and his entourage rushed for a meal before going to court. In his statement, the champion used his standard argument, no doubt raising eyebrows when in response to one question, said that he refused to take sides in the contest between communism and Christianity. The judge denied the restraining order.

Reporters followed Ali the rest of the day, peppering him with questions as he went to visit Texas Southern University, a predominantly black institution whose students cheered the champ. He urged them not to commit violence against whites. As to the prospect of jail, Ali responded that he had been "visiting prisons to get accustomed to them." He then puckishly added, "They say you're alright in them federal places. You can pay for your own food. You get TV. Only thing you don't get is your girlfriends" (Bingham and Wallace 150). He even tossed off a poem:

> He called the round when the clown hit the ground
> Tell little children whatever they believe,
> Stand up like Muhammad Ali. (Bingham and Wallace 150)

At 8:00 A.M. the next morning—30 minutes early—Ali arrived at the induction center. He easily passed the cursory physical exam, was given a box lunch (he tossed out the ham sandwich), and then at 1:05 P.M. entered the room where he would be inducted. The atmosphere was obviously electric. Outside, a few demonstrators carried signs that read, "We love Ali" and "Ali, stay home." One must have especially appealed to Ali's sense of humor: "Draft beer, not Ali" (Hauser 169). A few were more ominous. Some black students from Texas Southern carried a placard that indicated the kind of despair that Ali's plight engendered: "America is a house on fire. Let it burn, let it burn." And five black students did exactly that as they torched their draft cards (Bingham and Wallace 155). In the induction center, Lieutenant Steven S. Dunkley began reading names and inviting people to step forward to accept induction.[19] When he read Ali's name—"Cassius Marcellus Clay,"—of course, the champion stood still. When someone snickered, Dunkley ordered the room cleared—except for Ali. When ordered again, Ali refused a second time. A Naval officer, Clarence Hartman, took Ali to his office and explained the probable legal consequences of his actions: five years in prison and a $10,000 fine. Ali continued to refuse and finally was ordered to write out a statement confirming his decision. Ali said that he would not be inducted because he claimed an exemption as a Muslim minister. The commanding officer then took him to a crowded media room, where Ali distributed a lengthy statement, again outlining the reasons for his actions. He thanked supporters, then concluded, "If justice prevails,... I will be forced to go neither to the Army or jail. In the end I am confident that justice will come my way, for the truth must eventually prevail" (Hauser 170).

In retrospect, this was a seminal moment in American history. Perhaps the most well-known African American in the world risked his reputation, his career, and, given the vicissitudes of the prison environment, perhaps his life. Oddly, Ali himself didn't think that what he did was especially earth shattering: "I never thought of myself as great when I refused to go into the Army," he told Thomas Hauser. "All I did was stand up for what I believed" (Hauser 171). A small but increasing number of Americans were coming to a similar conclusion about the war and were standing up for their beliefs. It was perhaps no accident that a few weeks before Ali's fateful refusal to step forward, his only competitor for the honor of being the most famous African American in the world, Martin Luther King Jr., openly broke with the Johnson Administration regarding the war. On April 4, 1967, King told "an overflow crowd" at Riverside Church in New York that the Vietnam War was taking away resources from poor Americans "like some demonic, destructive suction tube" and that the United States government had become "the greatest purveyor of violence in the world today" (Wells 129). The war, finally, was wrong. Certainly, in April 1967, most Americans would disagree with King's and

Ali's views. But a tectonic shift was on the way. Within a few years the American people would be almost evenly divided in their view of the war. And, ironically, two of the most crucial, iconic leaders of those who came to oppose the war would be two African American ministers—a Baptist and a Muslim.

NOTES

1. Sonji told Thomas Hauser that Ali "was a good husband… . He's precious; he's sweet; he's gentle." Ali admits that when they separated, he "just about went crazy, sitting in my room, smelling her perfume." But, he concludes that "it was something that had to happen" because "she wouldn't do what she was supposed to do" (Hauser 130, 129). According to David Remnick, "All the non-Muslims" in the Ali entourage believed that the two "seemed to have a loving marriage which went wrong only when leaders of the Nation started putting pressure on Ali" (Remnick 270).

2. Ali's training was marred by a serious disagreement with his friend and resident clown, Bundini Brown. When Brown admitted that he had pawned Ali's championship belt, he was summarily dismissed, not to return officially to Ali's corner until later in his career.

3. Later, in a bizarre interview with journalist Gay Talese, Patterson said that he balked when Krause stopped the bout because he "was protesting stopping [Clay's] punches." As the champion landed more and more blows, Patterson said "a feeling of happiness came over me." He didn't want the fight to end because he "wanted to go out with a great punch, to go down that way" (Remnick 282). To be knocked out, it seems, would have mitigated the humiliation.

4. Ali and Patterson did not remain at odds, however. Not long after the fight, they met at a photo shoot for an article in *Esquire* magazine. Ali solicitously asked Patterson about the condition of his back, which had been injured in the bout. Patterson scolded reporters for being too hard on Ali. "He's only twenty-four years old, an entertainer, a very individualistic young man whose life is far from easy." He concluded that journalists should "make allowances for him." Ali reciprocated and told Patterson that he "should get honors and medals for the spot you was on, a good clean American boy fighting for America." Patterson responded with the ultimate compliment: he called the champion "Muhammad Ali" (Remnick 283). Much later, when Patterson was on the New York State Athletic Commission, he visited Ali's camp when he was training for a fight. They talked in private, and Patterson concluded that "he was a nice guy. I was surprised at how much I liked him. Believe it or not, he even seemed a little shy" (Hauser 141).

5. In an interesting footnote to the Patterson bout, when Ali was rejected by the two Robinsons, he then turned to Joe Louis. In January 1966, he announced that he had appointed the Brown Bomber as one of his advisers. Some observers, such as Wendell Smith, a black journalist, figured that "Cassius now wants to

improve his image." Donald McRae thinks that he also wanted to "[ease] Joe's financial burden," or maybe make Cassius Sr. happy. After all, the father "loved him [Louis]" more than the son did (McRae 330). Whatever the reasons for the choice, Louis lasted only three weeks. He continued to despise the NOI, but, perhaps more important, he was profoundly critical of Ali's boxing style. There couldn't be two Greatests in the same camp.

6. Members of the Ali entourage and friendly reporters such as Robert Lipsyte found the lowering of eligibility requirements deeply suspect. Howard Bingham argues that the draft pool was sufficiently deep in late 1965–early 1966 that the 30th percentile cutoff could have been sustained. Lipsyte said that "the change was suspicious to say the least" (Bingham and Wallace 112). It strains credulity (and suggests a certain level of paranoia in the Ali camp) to believe that the federal government would order such an alteration just to punish one man— even if he was "the Greatest."

7. There is considerable controversy over exactly what Ali said about the Viet Cong, the communist forces in South Vietnam. Lipsyte uses the "I ain't got no quarrel with" version in an interview with Thomas Hauser. Howard Bingham and Max Wallace, however, quote Lipsyte's notes differently: "I ain't got nothing against them Vietcong" (Bingham and Wallace 114). In his first autobiography, *The Greatest*, Ali goes with the "quarrel" version. He says that as he kept hearing the question, he characteristically, broke into verse: "Keep asking me, no matter how long/On the war in Vietnam, I sung this song/I ain't got no quarrel with the Viet Cong" (Ali, *The Greatest* 124).

8. Even the lawyer representing Ali's owners, the Louisville Sponsoring Group, showed grudging respect for his decision to oppose the war and to try to avoid military service, even such "cushy" duty in the National Guard, or putting on boxing exhibitions at military bases, as Joe Louis had done during World War II. Gordon Davidson said that such a stand was "to his credit.... This was a real point of principle for him and he wasn't about to make it easy on himself" (Remnick 288).

9. Interestingly, one of the (rather lame) reasons Clark gave was that Ali had "failed to sign his correct name [Cassius Clay]" on the license application (Hauser 146). The Clay/Ali conundrum wouldn't go away, and many Americans still refused to accept his Muslim name two years after he had adopted it.

10. The controversy followed Ali to Toronto when reporter Jerry Izenberg— generally an Ali fan—covered the fight. Izenberg said that he went to Canada to ask Ali a simple question: whether he planned to stay there after the fight. By 1966 an increasing number of antiwar Americans were crossing the border to escape conscription, and Izenberg wondered if Ali was going to follow suit. The champion replied indignantly: "America is my birth country. They make the rules, and if they want to put me in jail, I'll go to jail. But I'm an American and I'm not running away" (Bingham and Wallace 133).

11. Chuvalo certainly had stamina. Former champion Rocky Marciano once quipped, "If all fights were a hundred rounds, George Chuvalo would be unbeat-

en in any era" (Hauser 149). Ali would verify his opponent's toughness. After the fight, he noted, "Chuvalo's head is the hardest thing I ever hit" (Cassidy 58).

12. Cosell began an interview before the fight by intoning, "I am with Cassius Clay, also known as Muhammad Ali." In a poignant moment, Ali interrupted him, saying almost sadly, "Are you going to do that to me too?" Cosell promised the champion that he would never "do that again as long as I live. Your name is Muhammad Ali" (Hauser 157).

13. London's performance was so pathetic that when a courier gave the fighter's wife an envelope with his purse for the bout, she replied, "Oh, you mean they're giving it to 'im" (Cosell 205).

14. Mendel Rivers (D-S.C.), Chairman of the House Armed Services Committee and vociferous supporter of the war in Vietnam, told a Veteran of Foreign Wars convention in New York that he would urge a "complete overhaul" of the CO system if Ali's claim were upheld: "If that great theologian of Black Muslim power, Cassius Clay, is deferred," Rivers sarcastically shouted, "you watch what happens in Washington. We are going to do something if that [draft] board takes your boy and leaves Clay home to double talk" (Hauser 155).

15. Interestingly, U.S. Attorney Carl Walker believed that the board's decision to deny CO status was "political." He pointed out that this was "the only case I ever encountered where the hearing examiner recommended conscientious objector status and it was turned down." Walker believed that the government feared that if Ali won, he would set an example that might encourage other African Americans to refuse service. At this point, Ali knew that "he was left with only two choices—go into the army or go to jail" (Bingham and Wallace 131–32).

16. According to Thomas Hauser, the fight films are "inconclusive" on this issue (Hauser 163).

17. Bundini Brown later composed his own poetic tribute to this lady: "Miss Velvet Green/The evilest bitch I ever seen" (Ali, Greatest 163).

18. Ali's main counsel, Hayden Covington, was incensed at what he saw as government hypocrisy. He complained to his client, "[Football star] Joe Namath can get off to play football and [actor] George Hamilton gets out because he's going with the president's daughter, but you're different. They want to make an example of you" (Remnick 289).

19. Dunkley remembered clearly that the Pentagon was monitoring the whole ceremony and that "a lot of the guys who worked at the center were fans of Ali . . . [who] were excited" about his appearance (Bingham and Wallace 155).

Chapter 6

EXILE:
APRIL 1967–SEPTEMBER 1970

When Muhammad Ali stood still at his induction ceremony, he unleashed a series of consequences that were to have a major impact on his life and career. The first one came almost immediately. As he left the center, an elderly woman carrying an American flag approached him, screaming her venom: "You're heading straight for jail. You ain't no champ no more" (Wallace and Bingham 159). When Ali tried to answer, his lawyer shoved him into a cab.

An hour after his refusal, a harder blow fell. The New York State Athletic Commission suspended his boxing license in the state and refused to recognize his championship—all this before he'd even been charged with a crime. Marvin Kohn, the Commission's press secretary, vividly recalls the day. The chairman, Eddie Dooley, was a conservative Republican and former congressman who simply could not comprehend why Ali wouldn't do what Joe Louis had done in World War II: join the Army and put on boxing exhibitions for the troops. The Commission had an open line to the induction center. Kohn recalls that the three commissioners had already decided that Ali would lose his license and title in New York if he refused induction. When he did, Kohn "got on the phone and started calling the media" (Hauser 173). Dooley later explained to reporters that quite simply, "[Ali's] refusal to enter the service is regarded by the Commission as detrimental to the best interests of boxing" (Bingham and Wallace 160). The state athletic commissions in Texas and California followed New York's example, as did the World Boxing Association. Even the United Kingdom, where opinion over the Vietnam War was deeply divided, declared the heavyweight title vacant.

As might be expected, press reaction was hostile toward Ali. Milton Gross of the *New York Post* claimed that "Clay" had clearly become a religious fanatic. Gene Ward took Ali's decision personally and told his *New York Daily News* readers that he did not want his three sons ever to think that Ali was "any kind of hero." Indeed, he claimed he would "do anything to prevent it." Even the staid *New York Times*, whose support for the war had diminished throughout the years, weighed in editorially: "Citizens cannot pick and choose which wars they wish to fight in any more than they can pick and chose what laws they wish to obey." Surprisingly, much of the black press was also less than sympathetic. According to James Hicks in the *Louisville Defender*, "Clay should serve his time in the army just like any other healthy, All-American boy."[1] In an especially bizarre piece, black columnist Gordon Hancock complained that "we are bringing up a breed of 'womanish men' who are... draft dodgers... and mouthpieces for communism" (Gorn 139). But Louisville's major white newspaper delivered perhaps the cruelest blow. The sports editor of the *Courier-Journal* intoned with bitter sarcasm: "Clay is a slick opportunist who clowned his way to the top. Hail to Cassius Clay, the best fighter pound for pound that Leavenworth prison will ever receive" (Bingham and Wallace 161–62).

While the media firestorm raged around Ali, his legal team continued to try to have the Selective Service Board's decision reversed, claiming that his draft call was unconstitutional because there were very few African Americans serving on local boards in Kentucky. One of Ali's lawyers, Charles Morgan Jr., even asked for a restraining order that would stop the drafting of all African Americans. When these efforts failed, on May 8, 1967, Ali was indicted by a federal grand jury for refusal to be inducted into the armed services. He was freed on $5,000 bond.[2]

In an attempt to reach some sort of middle ground, Herbert Muhammad contacted former professional football star Jim Brown. Ali's NOI manager, who stood to lose a great deal of money if Ali went to jail, wanted Brown to meet with Ali to see if he would be willing to work out a deal with the Army. Herbert believed that the military would allow Ali to enter Special Services and entertain the troops with boxing exhibitions. Thus, he would not have to fight. (Herbert also insisted that Brown not tell Ali about his role in the affair.) In early June, Brown assembled 10 prominent black athletes to meet with Ali in Brown's Cleveland office to explore the possibility of such an arrangement. Among the luminaries were greats such as basketball stars Kareem Abdul-Jabbar from UCLA and Bill Russell of the Boston Celtics.[3] When some of the athletes told Ali that they believed he should accept some sort of noncombatant status, he stood firm: "I'm doing what I have to do" (Bingham and Wallace 173).[4]

The athletes who attended the meeting were enormously impressed by Ali's courage and sincerity. Jabbar recalls being "a hundred percent behind Ali," while Bill Russell was awed by what the young boxer did: "I was struck by how confident he was, how totally assured he was that what he was doing was right." Russell concluded, with great eloquence, that "philosophically, Ali was a free man,... one of the first totally free men in America" (Hauser, 178, 179).

These black athletes weren't the only Americans who stood behind Ali. Several liberal writers and supporters of Ali—among them George Plimpton, Norman Mailer, and Pete Hammil—met to form a kind of informal group to push for his reinstatement. Perhaps the strongest voice supporting Ali was that of Martin Luther King Jr. In a sermon on April 30, 1967, at Ebenezer Baptist, his home church in Atlanta, Dr. King continued his attack on the war. This time, however, he specifically referred to Ali. He praised the young fighter for his courage and sacrifice, giving up a potential fortune to stand by his principles. He urged other young men who opposed the war to see Ali as an example and follow his course of action. As for the charge that Ali was somehow a traitor, King replied said that any attempt "to equate dissent with disloyalty" was quite simply "dangerous." As for himself, King concluded, alluding to the old Protestant hymn: "I ain't going to study war no more." Interestingly, controversial Black Power advocate Stokely Carmichael was in King's audience, applauding enthusiastically. After the sermon, Carmichael exclaimed, "It's about time we're going to tell [the white man] 'Hell no, we won't go'" (Bingham and Wallace 166).

The voices of Jim Brown, King, Carmichael, and Plimpton, however, were drowned out by those who approved of the war. Especially disheartening to King, and to Ali, must have been the views of a number of African Americans, most of whom—around 60–65 percent—approved of the war in early 1967. The support was especially strong among black soldiers. Lieutenant Colonel Warren Kynard said that he didn't believe that "any American leader, black or white, can assist the cause of freedom by preaching the cause of sedition," thus, by implication, accusing Ali and King of treason (Bingham and Wallace 169, 168). This was especially ironic since Kynard was a friend of the King family and had once been engaged to Martin's wife, Coretta. Black combat medic Wayne Smith echoed the Colonel's sentiments. He recalled that his family taught him to "convince white Americans that blacks were as patriotic as they were." Ali made that job very difficult, and Smith said that "when

Ali came out against the war, I disagreed with him." Smith became especially incensed when he noted that Viet Cong soldiers left propaganda
leaflets lying around, supposedly quoting Ali: "BLACK SOLDIERS: NO
VIETNAMESE EVER CALLED YOU NIGGER" (Bingham and Wallace
169, 168). There is no firm evidence that Ali ever made this remark,
although it is often found conjoined with the "no quarrel" statement.[5]

Muhammad Ali went to trial on June 19, 1967, in an atmosphere that
was largely hostile to him. There was really no doubt as to the outcome.
Even Attorney General Ramsey Clark, a liberal who opposed the war and
personally believed that there should not be a religious test for conscientious objector (CO) status, admitted that Ali had no case based on law at
the time. U.S. Attorney Mort Susman cannily chose Carl Walker, a
young black assistant U.S. Attorney, to present the government's argument. Walker respected Ali because the champ wanted to cool the racial
tensions that surrounded the trial. There had been racial disturbances at
traditionally black Texas Southern University during the previous month
in which buildings were burned and one policeman was killed. Moreover,
rumors abounded that thousands of Black Muslims were planning to
descend on Houston to protest the trial. Ali quickly flew to Chicago to
urge members of the NOI not to hold a mass demonstration, and they
agreed.

After jury selection—six men and six women, all white—the actual
trial began on July 20 at 9:00 A.M. The trial ended nine hours later, and
the jury took only 21 minutes to arrive at a guilty verdict. When it was
announced, Howard Bingham noticed that Ali, who had been doodling
on a legal pad, "had drawn a picture of a plane crashing into a mountain"
(Bingham and Wallace 177). When Ali requested immediate sentencing,
Susman, who had been in the courtroom watching his young assistant
argue the case, said that he would not object if Ali received less than the
maximum sentence. But when he also claimed that he had studied the
NOI and found it to be "as much political as it is religious," Ali objected,
"If I can say so, sir, my religion is not political in any way" (Hauser 179).
Judge Joe Ingraham, known as a judicial conservative, ordered Ali to be
silent and then imposed the maximum sentence of five years in prison
and a $10,000 fine, and ordered Ali's passport confiscated.[6] Outside the
courtroom, Ali seemed unfazed as he told reporters, "I'm giving up my
title, my wealth, maybe my future. Many great men have been tested for
their religious belief. If I pass this test, I'll come out stronger than ever"
(Bingham and Wallace 178).

Part of that test would be watching his crown claimed by someone else.
The World Boxing Association (WBA), joined by Bob Arum, a former

Ali promoter and his newly formed Sports Action Inc., planned an elimination tournament among eight heavyweights to determine a new champion. ABC would broadcast the bouts. The New York State Athletic Commission sponsored a rival tournament under its auspices, so that the title was divided, with Joe Frazier defeating Buster Mathis for the New York title and Jimmy Ellis, Ali's former sparring partner, defeating Jerry Quarry for the WBA title. Ali was not impressed when he heard of the plans. In one of the most eloquent, humor-laced outbursts of his career, he exclaimed:

> Let them have the elimination bouts. Let the man that wins go to the backwoods of Georgia and Alabama or to Sweden or Africa. Let him stick his head in an elementary school. Let him walk down a back alley at night. Let him stop under a street lamp where some small boys are playing and see what they say. Everybody knows I'm the champion. My ghost will haunt all the arenas. I'll be there, wearing a sheet and whispering, "Ali—e-e-e!" "Ali—e-e-e!" (Hauser 181)

Ali's blast fell on deaf ears, of course, and no state commissions were moved to revisit their positions. In fact, many Americans believed that Ali had gotten off too easy when he was allowed to remain free while his lawyers appealed the court's decision. For some reason, much of the animus was directed at the ex-champ's local draft board even though it had no judicial powers. Said one irate citizen in a letter to board members: "Dear Skunks. You yellow bellied scum. You are as bad as those ... burning their draft cards," while another letter writer fumed, "That Black Bastard Cassius Clay should be in Vietnam right now" (Bingham and Wallace 179). Even President Lyndon Johnson got complaints that Ali wasn't either in Vietnam or locked up without bail.

Ali had actually gone to Los Angeles three days after the trial had ended to speak at an antiwar rally protesting President Johnson's appearance at a Democratic fund raising event. He told the crowd, "I am with you... . I'm not a leader... . But I encourage you to express yourself and to stop this war" (Bingham and Wallace 179). After his appearance, he watched Los Angeles police attack the demonstrators and injure more than 200. He decided not to participate in any more such rallies, in part, no doubt because the NOI discouraged its members from getting involved in issues that it perceived as white. He also worried that such participation would damage his chances in his appeals—one of which was to have his passport returned. In fact, the Los Angeles appearance did hurt his appeals. One judge ruled against Ali, saying that his speech in Los Angeles proved that "Mr. Clay demonstrates a ready willingness to participate in anti-government... activities" (Bingham and Wallace 182). And so in the weeks after his sentence, he essentially spoke at mosques and tried to keep his head down, at least for a while.[7]

In the midst of these legal and professional setbacks, Ali did find some personal happiness. He married a young member of the NOI, Belinda Ali (born Boyd). Traditionally, the story is that they met in a Muslim bakery in 1966, but actually Belinda recalls that she met Cassius Clay in 1961 at her Muslim school in Chicago, then a few years later at a Chicago Muslim convention. He had not fully converted, and she scolded him: "Your name is Clay. That means dirt. Why don't you get rid of your slave name" (Hauser 183). Ali kept in touch during the next couple of years and asked her to marry him when she was only 17 years old. Her mother, Aminah, worried that she was too young but refused to stop her. On August 17, 1967, they were married in a small private ceremony in Chicago. Belinda remembers that their early years were happy: "He taught me everything I knew, and in the beginning he was beautiful" (Hauser 185).

What was not so beautiful, however, was Ali's financial situation. Although he had grossed almost $4 million the ring and almost that much in endorsements, most of it was simply gone by the summer of 1967. Some obviously went to taxes and some to alimony payments for Sonji. His father, who never really accepted his son's conversion to Islam, thought that the NOI had pilfered much of it, but Ali denies this. His good friend Howard Bingham is convinced that Ali mainly gave his money away to his friends and supporters: "He cares so little for money and is so generous with what he does have that he has always been known as a soft touch..." (Bingham and Wallace 183). Sometimes he was simply taken, as when a retainer would double bill Ali and the NOI for expenses. Other times, he was achingly altruistic, as when he saved a man from jumping off a building, then bought him $1,800 worth of clothes to help him regain his dignity. By the summer of 1967, he was too broke to pay his lead attorney, Hayden Covington, the $247,000 that he still owed. Covington sued.

Ali was so desperate that he even signed on as a sparring partner for Joe Bugner, a British boxer preparing for a fight in the United States. Ali earned $1,000 and tried to cadge more by selling Bugner a special portable radio that Ali prized. That fall Ali turned to a Chicago businessman and friend, Eugene Dibble, who let him hang around his south-side garage and even take money from the cash register when he needed it. Although he continued to preach in the local Mosque, Ali was clearly bored and frustrated.[8] Dibble recognized that his friend needed something more to do, preferably an activity that would bring in some much needed cash.

Gene Dibble hit on a brilliant idea. Knowing how much Ali loved young people and how well they responded to him, Dibble took Ali to several local high schools and universities to speak to students. Although there was no money in these appearances, Ali was so skilled at communicating that word got out that he was a real presence. Around the same time, Jeremiah Shabbaz also arranged speaking engagements for Ali at Temple and at Cheyney State Universities for $1,500 each. Ali became well-known enough that he was wooed by two different professional agents and ultimately signed with Richard Fulton, Inc. Fulton sent out blizzard of flyers—more than 50,000—to schools, colleges, universities, and clubs all over the country, virtually any organization that might be able to use a charismatic speaker. He lined up enough appearances, especially at colleges and universities, that Ali could go on tour in late 1967.

The exiled Ali was both energized and intimidated by the prospect of a series of talks before college students. He told Thomas Hauser that he spent three months preparing for the tour. "I wrote all my ideas out on paper," then refined them, and "wrote them out again on note cards." He would then practice "in front of a mirror with Belinda listening." When he thought he was ready, he began the tour. As he recalled, "I must have gone to two hundred colleges, and I enjoyed the speaking. It made me happy" (Hauser 185).

As with most public speakers with strenuous schedules, there was often repetition in his speeches. For example, he would almost always end with a kind of call and response. Ali yelled out rhetorically, "Can my title be taken away without me being whipped?" The audience almost always responded, "No." Then Ali would whip them up further: "Who's the heavyweight champion of world?" A chorus of "you are's" would be followed by Ali: "One more time. We don't want no excuses. They might say the film in the camera was broke. Who's the champ of the world?" to which the audience would respond with a resounding, "You are!" (Bingham and Wallace 189).

But Ali also tried to vary his topics. He actually wrote six different speeches—probably more than most celebrities on the lecture circuit. He talked about familiar topics such as opposition to the war in Vietnam: "I'm expected to go overseas to help free people in South Vietnam, and at the same time my people here are getting brutalized." And "I'm just going to jail.... I'll face it before denouncing Elijah Muhammad and the religion of Islam." He also spoke a lot about black pride, and he complained about the pervasiveness of whiteness in popular culture: "White Owl cigars. White Swan soap. While Cloud tissue." He usually got a hearty laugh when he pointed out that "even Tarzan, the king of the jungle in Black Africa, he's white," and when he noted that "Angel food cake is white, but the devil's food cake is chocolate" (Hauser 188). Sometimes he would vary his topics according to the composition of the audience. According to Robert Lipsyte, in San Francisco, he launched into an attack on marijuana when the smell of pot wafted up from the audience. On another occasion, when he saw a number of racially mixed couples in the audience, he launched into a diatribe against intermarriage: "No... white man or white woman in his or her right mind wants [mixed marriages],... introducing their grand children as little mixed-up, kinky-headed, half-black niggers. You want your child to look like you" (Hauser 188). Such sentiments give some credence to the charge that his views mirrored those of the Ku Klux Klan.

In addition to reprising old ideas about war and race and boxing, Ali also spoke about more universal themes, a kind of "words of wisdom" approach. His homilies included pronouncements on personality—he said that humans weren't born with one. He talked about education, suggesting that "children go through three or four or five different colleges within themselves, even before they are three." As for friendship, he delivered the following bromide: "Whenever the thought of self-interest creeps in, that means the destruction of friendship" (Bingham and Wallace 188).

Most students listened politely to sentiments such as these, but what they really came for was the question-and-answer periods. These sessions generally got back to less trite and general topics than the meaning of friendship. To be sure, not all the questions and comments from the audience were supportive. Belinda recalls that he was sometimes heckled, called "draft dodging nigger," or something to that effect. On one occasion when Ali talked about quitting the tour because of such outbursts, Belinda encouraged him to "fight fire with fire." Later, when he was called exactly that—a draft dodging nigger—while talking at the University of Syracuse, he responded with a little story. His grandmother, Ali claimed, always told him never to throw stones at a donkey because the beast might come back to haunt him. Ali looked right at the heckler and concluded, "Ladies and gentlemen, I know now that my grandma was right because I believe that ass is in here tonight." His comment, Belinda remembers, "brought down the house," and he told the same story afterwards whenever he was heckled (Hauser 190).

When asked more politely about how he could condone fighting in the ring but not for his country, he pointedly responded that America only saw African Americans as citizens when they were draftable. He was often asked about hate and always responded that he didn't hate anyone. Once after lecturing at Harvard, he was even asked to compose, extemporaneously, a short poem. He responded without missing a beat: "Me. Whee!" (Ali, *Butterfly* 98). When queried at a Christian college about his religious sentiments, he responded poetically: "I used to be a Baptist. I used to wait for pie in the sky by and by. Now I want something sound on the ground while I am around" (Bingham and Wallace 190). How this mass of internal rime relates to Islamic theology isn't clear. When he did talk about his faith in Allah, he occasionally retained his sense of humor. Robert Lipsyte reports that Ali sometimes said, puckishly, "I ain't the Greatest no more because Allah is the Greatest. But I am still the prettiest" (Lipsyte 87). But when he turned to his faith, the preacher in him sometimes came out and he would scold students in the audience. Lipsyte thought it remarkable that when he did warn against "pre-marital sex and drugs to all these free love, pot smoking hippies,... they loved him." The main times his fans on the cultural left deserted him was when he would rant about interracial dating. Sometimes, an obviously mixed couple would launch a few catcalls, then leave the auditorium. There were also some hecklers when he would refer to Joe Frazier as a gorilla or make what even then were seen as sexist remarks about women's proper role.[9]

Nevertheless, in many ways, Ali became a shining example of courage to the antiwar movement and some elements of the civil rights movement, even though he never became an activist leader like Jerry Rubin or Martin Luther King Jr. African American opponent of the war, Julian Bond, recalls attending some of Ali's speeches. He "would have the crowd in the palm of his hand." Bond admitted that he was "crazy about Ali" (Hauser 186). Robert Lipsyte noted that "passionate young radicals regarded him as a hero" (Lipsyte 85). He concluded that Ali's speeches were "providing [young people] a window on a lot of social, religious, and political things that were going on in America" (Hauser 190). And Ali enjoyed the opportunity to speak: "During all the years I was away, I was never lonely... [while] meeting students and Black power groups and all the white hippies." Ali concluded that he "had a ball" (Bingham and Wallace 191).

There were a few other positive aspects of Ali's life during this period of exile. The birth of his daughter, Maryum, on June 18, 1968, certainly brightened his life. On the happy occasion, he quipped that he "gave up being the prettiest" (Lipsyte 87). In 1969, he had a role in a Broadway musical, *Big Time Buck White* by Oscar Brown. Although it closed rather quickly, Ali received passable reviews. Clive Barnes of the *New York Times* said he moved "with innate dignity," concluding that he "[did] himself proud" (Hauser 197). He also had a role in a documentary film, called *A/K/A Cassius Clay*, for which he was paid $7,000. He was even able to get back into the ring, at least in a virtual sense. Bert Sugar and a computer aficionado named Murray Woroner inputted Ali's statistics and those of ex-champ Rocky Marciano into a computer and generated several scenarios. They then arranged for the two to get in the ring and go through the motions of a fight—in 75 one-minute rounds—so the computer fight could seem to be real and shown on closed circuit television. In the version shown in the United States, Marciano knocked out Ali in the 13th round. Incensed by the results, European theaters showed a different version in which Marciano lost by a TKO.[10] According to Howard Bingham, Ali "would always regret" the Marciano project, perhaps because of the way anti-Ali newspapers gloated over the American results. Said the *Philadelphia Inquirer*: "A loud mouthed black racist... [had] his ass whipped"—if only in virtual reality (Bingham and Wallace 217, 218).

Perhaps one of the greatest comforts to Ali during his exile was his growing friendship with Howard Cosell. The broadcaster had first met Ali as Cassius Clay in August 1962, then interviewed him after he returned from the first Cooper fight in 1963. They almost immediately struck up a relationship based on a combination of banter and respect. Ali mocked Cosell when he thought Liston would crush him, and by mid-1964 Ali began a series of interviews on ABC. At his training camp before the second Liston fight, Ali grabbed Cosell in a mock headlock and screamed, "Stop, everybody, this is Howard Cosell. And I'm gonna whup him. He thinks Sonny Liston can beat me"—a refrain that became an Ali mantra when they would appear in public (Cosell 190). In both 1965 and 1966, Cosell interviewed Ali a number of times, and they continued to kid each other. Cosell was actually in Ali's hotel room the night before his aborted induction. Cosell was amazed at how calm the champ was, as he lay "in bed watching Johnny Carson, the bed sheets tucked under his chin" (Cosell 214–15). On the next day, Ali allowed Cosell to read his statement (to be shown on ABC) and agreed that it was an accurate statement of his beliefs, even though Elijah had told Ali not to talk to the media about his political stand. And when state boxing commissions stripped Ali of his license, Cosell also recalls how angry he was at the decision. Years later, Cosell told Thomas Hauser that these commissioners were "nothing but a bunch of politically appointed hacks" and that he still got "furious" about the fact that Ali was not allowed to fight in any state "and that piece of scum [boxing promoter] Don King has not been barred by one" (Hauser 173).[11]

During the next two and a half years, Cosell stood by Ali. He attended one of the performances of *Buck White,* coincidentally sitting next to Floyd Patterson. Ali spied Cosell, and while taking his bows tossed a few quips at the sportscaster, noticed Patterson, and said, "My friend, Floyd Patterson, has come to see me" (Cosell 219). Cosell also shared Ali's fascination with Jack Johnson.

Of course, Ali might well have been a bit disingenuous, even self-protective when he claimed that his life in exile was not so bad and that he had a ball on his lecture tour. In spite of his success as a speaker and his hero status among those who opposed the war, his time away from fighting was a bitter pill to swallow. He was kept under constant surveillance by the FBI. Even the U.S. Army Intelligence and Security Command had him shadowed. A typical report by an agent, dated May 21, 1968, had "Clay" arriving in St. Louis, going to a night club, attending a Black Muslim convention where he "spoke for 45 minutes, mostly about himself and his cause, which is to avoid being placed in a white man's army" (Hauser 191). He even spent some time in jail, although not because of his stance on the war. In December 1968, he was sentenced in Dade County, Florida, to 10 days incarceration for driving without a valid license. His lawyer figured he had to do time for an offense usually settled with a fine simply because of who he was. Ali recalls the time in jail with great distaste: "The food is bad, and there's nothing good to do. You look out the window... , and everyone else seems so free." Nonetheless, Ali maintains, he was ready to spend five years in prison if he had to go (Hauser 192).

But perhaps the greatest blow was his suspension from the Nation of Islam. In April 1969, during an appearance on ABC's *Wide World of Sports,* Ali said that he would love to fight again "if the money was right." Elijah Muhammad, watching from his palatial Chicago home, was furious. He ordered that Ali be suspended from the NOI for a year because he seemed more interested in the white man's money that in serving Allah. *The Messenger* published the ban in its April 4, 1969, issue.[12] According to Ali's friend, Eugene Dibble, the young fighter was devastated. "He acted like a little boy who had been spanked for being bad" (Bingham and Wallace 211). Although Ali was clearly disturbed by the suspension, he saw it as a test from Allah and continued to praise Elijah in his speeches. Because he seemed to be showing real remorse, Herbert

Muhammad ultimately convinced his father not to specifically condemn Ali's attempts to fight again. But Elijah was still not happy. Indeed, Ali's name wasn't mentioned in *The Messenger* for three more years.

Ali's legal fortunes weren't much better in 1968–1969 than his religious ones. In May 1968, the U.S. Court of Appeals upheld his conviction, and in March 1969, the Supreme Court refused to hear the case. However, a ray of light appeared a few days later when the Court discovered that illegal wiretaps might have played a role in the trial, and it returned the case to a lower court. Unfortunately for Ali, a federal district court ultimately ruled that the tapes were not crucial to his conviction and once again upheld the sentence. Ali's last chance would come on a reappeal to the Supreme Court, which would probably not rule until early 1971.

One positive note from 1969 was a vast improvement in his financial situation. Chauncey Eskridge, one of Ali's lawyers, made a deal in which a business group would use Ali's name and likeness to sell "Champburger" franchises. For this deal, Ali received $900,000. A week later, he scored a $200,000 publisher's advance for his autobiography, *The Greatest*. Faced with the anger of his spiritual leader and the seeming hopelessness of his legal appeals, Ali now believed he had the funds to quit the game. He told *Esquire Magazine* that he was done with boxing. In an article, boldly entitled "I'm Sorry, but I'm Through Fighting Now," he suggested that he wanted to spend the rest of his life helping the poor. He did admit that he might consider a few exhibition bouts in which he would whip heavyweight champion Joe Frazier if the gate went to Ali's new cause: wiping out poverty. Indeed, he hoped to set up a foundation to help him achieve this lofty goal, but, as Eugene Dibble says, legal fees and administrative costs sapped most of his funds. As Dibble put it, "The vultures came right out of the woodwork" (Bingham and Wallace 221).

In the meantime, key members of Ali's entourage were less than thrilled by their hero's philanthropic impulses. They were trying to find a place for him to fight. Herbert Muhammad made a bizarre attempt to convince an Indian tribe in Arizona to provide a venue because reservations did not require a boxing commission's sanction. The Tribal Council balked, claiming that such a brutal sport would desecrate sacred ground. Publicist Harold Conrad, a long-time member of the Ali entourage, had no better luck. He struck out in California, allegedly was told he needed to grease palms in Montana, and was stymied by the mob in Las Vegas. Tijuana, Mexico, was willing, but the U.S. government wouldn't allow Ali to leave the country.

But in early 1970, Ali, less flush with cash and more receptive to the lure of the ring, received a call from Leroy Johnson, an influential African American state senator from Atlanta. Because Georgia had no state boxing commission, individual cities could sanction bouts. Johnson had delivered enough black votes to secure the recent Atlanta mayoral election for Sam Massell, a relatively liberal white politician. Calling in his chips, Johnson convinced a somewhat reluctant Massell to approve a bout that featured Ali. Initially, there were hopes that reigning champ Joe Frazier would be the opponent, but he refused. So promoters chose a young white hope, Jerry Quarry. Governor Lester Maddox, a rabid segregationist most famous for using a pickaxe to drive away blacks who tried to eat at his restaurant, was livid. But ultimately all he could do legally was call for a day of mourning in Georgia when the papers for the fight were signed, and urge Atlantans to boycott it. And although several Congressmen and other national officials complained, the fight would take place on October 26, 1970. Muhammad Ali was about to emerge at least partially, from the wilderness.

NOTES

1. This sort of comment is emblematic of the relative conservatism of the black press on this issue. Hicks referred to Ali as Clay, as did almost all white reporters—except Howard Cosell. And one can imagine the uproar today if any media outlet called a 26-year-old black man "boy."

2. As part of the bail agreement, Ali promised not to leave the country. This effectively eliminated any opportunity to fight professionally while his case dragged on. Some Islamic countries still recognized him as world champion, but he could not use them as a venue for prizefighting.

3. Others at the meeting were pro football players Bobby Mitchell, Jim Shorter, Willie Davis, John Wooten, Sid Williams, Walter Beach, and Curtis McClinton.

4. Actually Brown knew that Ali wouldn't change his mind because when he met with Ali privately the night before, Ali remained adamant. There is still much confusion about the role of the NOI and Elijah Muhammad in the draft controversy. In his most recent memoir, Ali claims that "even the Nation of Islam tried to persuade me to accept induction" (Ali, *Butterfly* 87). So at some point Ali must have learned of Herbert's phone call to Brown. Jeremiah Shabbaz, Ali's friend and spiritual mentor from back in Miami, tells a different story. He says that no one connected with the NOI put pressure on Ali in any way. Elijah himself told reporters in regard to Ali and the draft, "Every one of my followers is free to make his own choice" (Bingham and Wallace 145). Historian David K. Wiggins points out that Elijah talked openly about the case and criticized the

government for harassing Ali. Nonetheless, he was "careful not to incriminate himself in any wrongdoing" (Gorn 100). Perhaps the most compelling evidence that the NOI was involved is Jim Brown's testimony in addition to Ali's own memory. In all likelihood, the NOI did try to convince Ali to serve but not in combat.

5. Historian Thomas Hietala quotes black militant Stokely Carmichael as saying in 1966, "We [African Americans] ain't going to Vietnam. Ain't no Vietcong ever called me nigger" (Gorn 139). This may be the genesis of the statement.

6. Ingraham said later that although Ali "was a nice, polite, well-behaved young man,... I gave him the sentence that I did because that's what he deserved" (Hauser 180).

7. The FBI certainly still saw Ali as a threat. A July 25 memo to Director Hoover from one of the agents assigned to investigate Ali said that "Clay" used public appearances "to promote... an ideology completely foreign to the basic American ideals of equality and justice for all" (Hauser 191).

8. Howard Bingham speculates that much of Ali's discontent grew from the fact that he hated "the idea of giving up his place on the national stage," mainly because the celebrity status "served to fuel his remarkable, gregarious personality." In late 1967, it was not unusual for local denizens of Chicago to see Ali walking down the sidewalks, arms in the championship position over his head, shouting "good naturedly, 'Who's the greatest around here? I'm looking for a fight'" (Bingham and Wallace 186, 187).

9. According to Julian Bond, some conservative black civil rights activists were horrified by Ali. They believed his faith and his opposition to the war would alienate President Johnson and hurt the cause of black equality (Hauser 186).

10. Marciano never learned of either result because he died in a plane crash three days after the bout was filmed.

11. According to George Plimpton, Cosell at the time was not willing to go very far out on a limb for Ali. Plimpton went to Cosell's office at ABC to urge him to join the committee of writers who wanted a reinstatement of the title. He recalls Cosell's reaction: "Georgie-boy, I'd be *shot*, sitting right here in this armchair by some crazed redneck sharpshooter... if I deigned to say over the airwaves that Muhammad Ali should be... allowed to return to the ring" (Plimpton 136). Reporter Larry Merchant thinks Cosell was worried about "jeopardizing his position at ABC," which "at the time... was a very conservative network" (Bingham and Wallace 165). Clearly, however, Cosell soon became a fervent proponent of Ali's right to fight.

12. There is considerable controversy regarding Elijah's motives in banning Ali. Jeremiah Shabbaz claims that Elijah "didn't want to be involved with anyone who was so weak as to go crawling on hand and knees to the white man for a little money" (Hauser 194). Elijah's biographer, Claude Clegg, doesn't buy this official explanation. After all, the NOI condoned Ali's taking white people's

money for five years prior. More likely, as with Malcolm X, Elijah was jealous of Ali's growing name recognition and international popularity. According to Clegg, he may also have figured that "in the era of Black Power, the boxer was no longer an essential factor in the appeal of the Nation to young African Americans" (Bingham and Wallace 211). David Wiggins proposes the intriguing argument that Elijah was simply trying to "ensure a public image for Ali that fit [Elijah's] own needs." He wanted Ali to be seen as a Muslim who happened to fight, not a fighter who happened to be a Muslim (Gorn 104). Whatever the truth, Elijah's motives were no doubt complex.

Chapter 7

A TRIUMPHANT RETURN: OCTOBER 1970–JANUARY 1974

Muhammad Ali's return from exile in the bout against Jerry Quarry did not occur in a vacuum. Although a majority of Americans probably still found much in Ali's religious faith unpalatable and his stance against the Vietnam War unacceptable, by 1970 millions of other Americans were growing increasingly disillusioned by that conflict. The Tet Offensive in 1968 had suggested to many that President Johnson had not told the truth about alleged progress in the war. Richard Nixon was elected president in 1968 partly because he promised to work for peace with honor. And although his policy in Vietnam in one sense continued the carnage, his strategy of Vietnamization did lead to a massive reduction of U.S. troops, which began in 1970. Indeed, in that year, a Gallup Poll showed that by a 56–36 percent margin, Americans believed that "the United States made a mistake sending troops to fight in Vietnam" (Gallup 2254). It seems that more and more Americans were coming to share Ali's opinions of the war.

Anecdotal evidence also suggests a certain mellowing in attitude toward the former champ. While one might expect antiwar senators such as Bobby and Ted Kennedy to praise Ali—Teddy said that "[Ali's] actions contributed enormously to the debate" about the war and that Ali had "galvanized some of his admirers to join protests against the war"—even some in the heartland began to notice that Ali might well have done the right thing. Famed Penn State football coach, Joe Paterno, for example, told Thomas Hauser that the stand Ali took on the draft was "what spoke most about him, that... [he was] a man of great principle."[1] Likewise, prolific author James Michener, whose 1971 book on the Kent State shootings essentially blamed the student demonstrators, not the National Guard, for the tragedy, nonetheless said that he became "an unqualified admirer" of Ali. Although Michener fought in World War II even though he was a Quaker, he believed that Ali's stand showed that the young boxer had a kind of courage that Michener did not. He concluded that "within his milieu, Ali was brilliant" (Hauser 199, 200, 201).

Such positive sentiments helped build the hype for the Ali–Quarry bout. And no doubt so did continued negative feelings about Ali on the part of many. The former champ received a number of threats. On the night before he was to leave for Atlanta, Ali opened a gift-wrapped box that contained a Confederate flag and a black Chihuahua with its head severed. Not long after he arrived in Atlanta, Ali was awakened by gunshots outside Senator Johnson's home, where he was staying. Shortly after, an anonymous caller told him, "Nigger,... You Viet Cong bastard. Next time we won't miss" (Bingham and Wallace 228). And, of course, Governor Maddox continued to rail against Ali and the bout.[2] So great was the interest that huge ticket sales led to the largest purse that Ali had received to that point.

On the night of the fight, Ali supporters dominated the crowd. Bert Sugar, the publisher of *Boxing Illustrated,* recalls seeing Ali ascend to his hotel room in a glass elevator, while in the lobby below throngs of supporters cheered. Said Sugar, "It was spine tingling; it transcended anything I'd ever seen" (Hauser 210). The spectators in the arena where the fight took place were 90 percent black, almost all screaming for Ali. Quarry claimed that the overwhelming sentiment for Ali didn't bother him, and he refused to turn the bout into some kind of racial metaphor: "I wasn't fighting for any race, creed, or color. I was fighting for money,... [not] against a symbol" (Hauser 211).

Although Ali clearly won the 1st round, in the second Quarry landed a thunderous hook to the body; Ali looked like he was in for a real challenge. But in the 3rd round, the former champ opened an enormous cut over Quarry's eye, exposing the bone beneath it. Ignoring Quarry's objections, referee Tony Perez stopped the fight. Although there were rumblings that Ali had actually used an illegal head butt to disable his opponent, Quarry disagreed, saying simply, "It was a right hand" (Hauser 212).

Although Ali's fans were overjoyed by the triumphant return, there were nagging concerns in his camp. To be sure, he seemed even stronger than ever. But he was also not as quick of foot as he had been prior to his forced layoff. Ali's doctor, Ferdie Pacheco, worried especially about his fighter's legs. Before the exile, Ali "[had] been so fast, you couldn't catch him"—save for a handful of lucky punches from the likes of Henry Cooper. But with three and a half years outside the ring, Pacheco quoted the old saying that "the legs are first to go" (Hauser 213).

Of course, Ali's people wanted his next fight to be held in the in the Mecca of boxing, New York City's Madison Square Garden. His lawyers, aided by the National Association for the Advancement of Colored People's (NAACP) Legal Defense Fund, came up with a strategy to have Ali's New York license reinstated. NAACP attorneys discovered that the State Athletic Commission had restored boxing licenses to dozens of convicted felons, including rapists and murderers. In September 1970, they successfully argued in District Court that continuing to deprive Ali of the right to fight in New York was illegal because it discriminated against him and violated his Fourteenth Amendment rights. The judge who ruled in the case called the commission's original decision "astonishing... , arbitrary, and unreasonable" (Hauser 214). Ali had his New York license and was looking for Joe Frazier.

On the way to his bout with Frazier, however, Ali stumbled through a warm-up fight against the hard-hitting, unorthodox Argentine heavyweight, Oscar Bonavena. Nicknamed "Ringo" because of his Beatles-like haircut, Bonavena was a tough customer. He won 59 fights in his career—42 by knockout—while losing only nine. The losses included two monumental battles with Joe Frazier. In the first, in 1966, he decked Frazier twice in the 1st round, only to lose in the final round. In the second match, a WBA title fight two years later, he took the champ the full 15 rounds. Ali looked uninspiring to say the least in New York in December 1970 when he took on Oscar. For the first 14 rounds, the Argentine held his own, even hurting the ex-champ in the 9th round. Ali responded by mocking his style and provoked Bundini Brown, who was again in Ali's corner, to yell, "Box like Sugar Ray. Get vicious." Ali responded between rounds by offering to give Bundini his gloves and have a go: "I don't know what to do with the clumsy fool" (Kram 104). He figured it out in the 15th round, however, pounding Oscar with a vicious left hook to the chin as the Argentine was looking up at the balcony for some mysterious reason. The referee stopped the fight.

Joe Frazier happened to be in the audience with his manager Yank Durham. As the fight progressed, and Ali seemed less and less formidable, Frazier began to worry. After all, if Ali lost, a potential Frazier–Ali bout worth a lot of money might be called off. Frazier said to Yank, "If [Ali] keeps foolin' with that bowling ball [Bonavena], we could lose millions." At one point, according to Durham, "Joe damn near jumped in the ring himself." But as Oscar collapsed, Frazier quietly said, "Now he's mine" and refused to go into the ring to congratulate his next opponent: "I got nuthin' to say to that clown" (Kram 104). In a few months his fists would do the talking in the first battle of one of the greatest rivalries in sports history.

Joseph William Frazier was born in Beaufort, South Carolina, on January 12, 1944, the 12th of 13 children of Rubin Frazier, a sharecropper. Much like Sonny Liston, Joe was on his own by the time he reached the age of 15. He dropped out of school after the 9th grade and moved to New York City to live with an older brother. Similar to Liston, he wound up on the wrong side of the law when he began stealing cars. Soon, however, before the New York police could catch him, Joe moved to Philadelphia to live with other relatives. He wanted to see if his luck would improve. He worked at a slaughterhouse and honed his incipient boxing skills by pounding on the sides of meat.[3] Joe eventually found his way to a gymnasium that was run by the police department, much like Ali, where he learned the science of prizefighting. Boxing changed his life. As an amateur, he lost in the Olympic qualifying round to Buster Mathis and became his sparring partner. When Mathis broke his hand on Joe's head, Joe stepped in to win the Olympic Gold Medal in the heavyweight division, just as Ali had done as a light heavyweight. Joe turned professional in 1965 and embarked on a remarkable career. He won his first 11 fights by knockouts, with none going past the 6th round. In 1968, he knocked out Buster Mathis in the 11th round to win the New York State heavyweight title. In February 1970, he won the World Boxing Association world heavyweight championship from Jimmy Ellis, thus unifying the New York and WBA titles, and defended it against Bob Foster in November. Like Ali, he was undefeated.

Frazier also followed Ali's career with profound interest. He watched Ali's fights and prefight shenanigans. He told writer Stephen Brunt that Ali "had lots of lips," which Frazier found offensive. After hearing Cassius try to humiliate Sonny Liston, Frazier recalled thinking, "I'm going to close his mouth" (Brunt 113).

Joe liked Ali's stand on the draft even less than he cared for his lip. Interestingly, Joe failed the same selective service test that Ali did and, like Ali, was later reclassified as acceptable for military service. Unlike Ali, however, Joe said that he actually wanted to serve in the military: "I loved the armies and navies and air force and marines," he told Stephen Brunt (Brunt 113). And he was acutely disappointed when he initially failed. But he realized that he needed money to support his family, so he grudgingly accepted a draft deferment because he was married with children.

Even though he didn't serve, Frazier still condemned Ali for failing to do so: "Of course he was wrong," Frazier insisted. "I didn't even have to think about that." Frazier realized that Ali would not even have had to serve in combat (as Frazier no doubt would have if he had been drafted in the mid-1960s). Ali had missed a golden opportunity to entertain the troops—both black and white. In Frazier's view, this would have "[brought] people together,... served the country" (Brunt 114). Instead, Ali became a martyr and a hero to the antiwar movement. To Joe, that was a travesty: "He's no martyr. The heroes are them kids with their pieces of body all over Vietnam, [including] a lot of poor blacks" (Kram 130).

Interestingly, Frazier and Ali actually had contact with each other several times after Ali was stripped of his title. They first met in 1968; then a year later Ali went to Philadelphia, where Frazier was headquartered, and convinced him to stage a mock fight in the gym where the new champ trained. Frazier went along with the idea in part because he realized the publicity value if Ali were allowed to fight him someday. Sadly, Ali was still the great draw while Frazier believed people saw him as an accidental champion, the beneficiary of Ali's defiance of the government. But there was also an element of compassion. Frazier rode with Ali to New York once and even lent him money. More significantly, he lobbied vigorously to get Ali's license restored. He even recalls meeting with President Nixon to plead Ali's case—and by extension, his own.[4]

Once Ali's ban was lifted, Joe Frazier was grimly determined to teach him a lesson. As he recalled to Stephen Brunt, "Nineteen seventy-one was the year. I made that New Year's resolution that I was going to dust that butterfly off. I was going to clip his wings." To Frazier it wasn't a question of money. It was pride, his overwhelming desire to "show [Ali] who was the greatest" (Brunt 117). Poignantly, the poor kid from South Carolina wanted to arrogate to himself Ali's self-appointed epithet and be "the greatest."

On December 30, 1970, Ali and Frazier signed the agreement to fight. Los Angeles talent agent Jerry Perrenchio and multimillionaire sportsman Jack Kent Cooke agreed to pay the two fighters $2.5 million each, without having ever met them. Madison Square Garden would provide the venue. The bout itself, and the hoopla leading up to it was "the biggest event in the history of boxing" (Hauser 217). Journalist Mark Kram noted that Ali, as might be expected, spared no hyperbole in his assessment. He claimed that as a result of the fight "the planet would stumble in its axis, billions would hold their breaths, including every last ice-covered Sherpa and sand-swept Bedouin" (Kram 127).

Ali did all he could to hype the bout, as he launched a series of verbal assaults against Frazier reminiscent of his attacks on Floyd Patterson. Early on in his training, from the relative security of the 5th Street Gym, he taunted Frazier for his alleged provincialism. Frazier was "a little nigger boy who ain't been anywhere 'cept Philly,... never had a thought in his dumb head except about himself" (Kram 128). Later he asserted that Frazier was "to ugly to be champ, too dumb." Were Frazier ever asked how it felt to be champ, Ali concluded, "he'll say, 'duh, duh, duh'" (Hauser 221)

What nettled Frazier the most, however, was Ali's claim that somehow Frazier had become a stooge for white people who hated African Americans. Dave Wolf, former sports editor of *Life Magazine* and a member of Frazier's camp, recalls once when he and Frazier watched Ali on a television talk show in the run up to the fight. Ali claimed that "the only people rooting for Joe Frazier were white people in suits, Alabama sheriffs, and members of the Ku Klux Klan." He went on to maintain that he, Ali, was "fighting for the little man in the ghetto." Frazier bridled at this notion, recognizing that Ali's middle-class background was far removed from black poverty. "What does he know about the ghetto?" Frazier raged, as he "[sat] there smashing his fist into his hand" (Hauser 219).

Ali's drumbeat of accusations that Frazier was an Uncle Tom had some no doubt unintended but ugly consequences. Frazier's son, Mavis, was tormented in school, and anonymous phone calls repeated the Uncle Tom charge. Some callers even threatened Frazier's life should he defeat Ali. The paranoia in the Frazier camp became so powerful that police guarded him around the clock. And when he broke training camp to go to New York City, five detectives joined the entourage to protect the champion.

Nonetheless, Ali kept up the assault in his usual fashion, combining the macho attacks associated with assertive manhood with the puckish humor of someone who was still a kid at heart. He claimed that as Frazier arrived at the ring, he would "feel like a traitor" when he realized how few blacks supported him. If by some miracle Frazier won, Ali claimed, "Only Nixon will call him," an unpopular president congratulating an unpopular fighter. In a burst of exaggeration, Ali demanded that 15 referees be in the ring because "there ain't no one man who can keep up with the pace I'm gonna' set except me." He went so far as to claim that the fight was so important that "Egypt and Israel will declare a forty-five minute truce" during the bout. "Not since time began has there been a night like this." And, of course, he wrote a poem proclaiming that he would win: "Joe's gonna' come out smokin'/But I ain't gonna' be jokin'/I'll be pickin' and pokin'/Pouring water on his smokin'" (Hauser 221, 223).[5]

Thomas Hauser got it right when he said of the first Ali–Frazier fight: "On March 8, 1971, the eyes of the world were focused on a small square of illuminated canvas, which had become one of the great stages of modern times" (Hauser 225). Madison Square Garden was sold out, with more than 20,000 fans expected at the bout. Thirty-five foreign countries ranging from England to Yugoslavia paid for the rights to show the fight via satellite. Almost 400 venues throughout the United States and Canada would show the bout on closed-circuit television, with tickets selling from 10 to 35 dollars. Garden officials handed out 760 press passes and, according to publicist John Condon, "turned down requests for 500 more." One reporter from Israel told Condon that his 80-year-old mother had asked him at breakfast one morning, "Who's going to win, Ali or Frazier?" a clear symbol of the international resonance of a mere prizefight (Hauser 221–22).

In his dressing room Ali both joked and mock taunted. He puckishly tried to guess on what part of his person Pat Patterson, Ali's personal bodyguard, was hiding his weapon, while teasing Bundini Brown for being incomprehensible. The taunting became more serious when Butch Lewis, a member of the Frazier retinue, came to monitor the taping of Ali's hands.[6] Ali "shot up from the table, started to pirouette through the room with a volley of punches. He shouted to Lewis, 'Take this back to your dumb chump'" (Kram 139).

Frazier's dressing room was less crowded and more calm. Frazier's manager assured him that he was ready for the fight. Five minutes before leaving, Frazier went to his knees and prayed for divine protection: "God let me survive this night. God protect my family. God grant me strength. And God... allow me to kick the s[—] out of this mutha[—]" (Kram 140).

Students of boxing agree that what happened in the next 45 minutes was one of the jewels in the history of the sport. Two superb, confident heavyweights had at it for 15 rounds. Although Ali might have been the master of the psyche out, Frazier was simply the superior fighter that night. The bout was even the first few rounds. Ali tried to end it early while Frazier kept boring in, legs and arms working like pistons. Although Ali was four inches taller and nine and a half pounds heavier than Joe, Frazier was able to hit Ali more often and harder than any opponent ever had before. In the middle rounds, Ali spent considerable time on the ropes, resting, while Frazier piled up points that would be crucial in the later judging. Ali also tried to whip the champ with his tongue, screaming as Frazier bore in: "Don't you know that I'm God?" (Kram 144).

By the 15th round, Ali was exhausted, still reeling from a massive Frazier hook in the 11th. Knowing that he was probably behind, Ali showed one final burst, snapping Frazier's head back in the first few seconds of the round with solid jabs. Then, finding an opening, Frazier landed a devastating left hook that lifted Ali off his feet. Stumbling backwards, he landed on the canvas in a daze. Ferdie Pacheco thought it was the hardest left hook Frazier had ever thrown and was convinced Ali would never get up. But he did in an act so courageous that referee Arthur Mercante decided that Ali was "the most valiant fighter" he had ever seen (Hauser 229). Ali finished the fight standing.

The outcome was hardly in doubt. Joe Frazier won a unanimous decision, with the two judges calling it a clear victory, 9-6 and 11-4. Mercante saw it as closer, 8-6-1, more an Ali defeat for staying too long on the ropes than a Frazier victory. The favored and favorite of millions had lost his first professional fight.

Despite the decision, Ali's friend, Howard Cosell, an astute judge of prizefighting, concluded in 1974 that "it might have been the greatest fight Ali ever fought." After all, he had lost almost four prime fighting years and was clearly not as fast on his feet as he had been. Frazier was probably the best boxer he had ever faced, and Ali finished the bout on his feet. In addition, according to Cosell, he "had inflicted untold physical damage upon Frazier, who ever since that day [showed] no sign of being the very good fighter he had been." That fight of the century "was an authentication of Ali's greatness as a fighter" (Cosell, 234).[7]

Ali was both whiny and gracious in defeat. In a press conference the next day, he implied that the decision had been a bad one. And even if it wasn't, he argued that he had only trained for a six-round fight. He said that had he been younger, he would have been able to dance away from Frazier's relentless pressure—"Joe stayed on me, always on my chest," he admitted. And he also agreed with Mercante that he lost some rounds by staying on the ropes to save energy. Nonetheless, Ali concluded that he "didn't give [the fight] away. Joe earned it." He waxed almost philosophical about the loss: "There are more important things to worry about," he mused. "Plane crash, ninety people die.... Presidents get assassinated." Those are crucial events, more so than a mere defeat in the ring. "The world goes on," he concluded (Hauser 231, 233).[8]

Frazier was less civil in victory. Even years later, he told Thomas Hauser that he "never liked Ali... except [sometimes] if we was alone and he was talking about the wife and kids." He hated the mouth, the needling, the adolescent bantering. "I was mad as a junkyard dog at Ali." In thinking about the fight, Frazier concluded, "Let Clay do the talking. All I had to do was punch" (Hauser 232). Frazier also believed, perhaps mistakenly, that many people in the audience wanted to see him demolish Ali. Certainly, Ali's old nemesis Red Smith felt vindicated: "Joe Frazier would whip Muhammad Ali a dozen times; and it would get easier as they went along" (Hauser 232). Seldom had a journalistic prognostication been so wrong.[9]

If the loss to Frazier was a bitter disappointment, on June 28, 1971, Ali experienced a major victory of another sort. The U.S. Supreme Court threw out his conviction for refusing induction into the armed forces. In a complicated set of maneuvers, the Court ruled on the basis of a technicality, in essence claiming that the Justice Department had misled the Louisville Selective Service Board about federal standards for denying conscientious objector status. Six justices agreed that Ali's religious beliefs were sincere and that the Kentucky Board erred in not taking this fact into consideration. Two others concurred on other grounds, which resulted in an 8–0 decision in Ali's favor.[10] Because he had passed the legal draft age of 26, Ali did not need to register again. Ali found out about the decision as he stopped at a Chicago orange juice stand. A man ran up to him, shouting, "I just heard it on the radio. The Supreme Court said you're free" (Freedman 79). Ali's reaction was subdued. He described his emotions as "blank," suggesting that he wouldn't really feel free until he traveled "to foreign countries [to] see all those strange people on the streets" (Hauser 239). He even forgave the government officials and judges who ruled against him, refusing to blame them for doing what they thought was legally correct. But in truth, a great weight had been lifted, and Ali could pursue something the courts could not grant him: the heavyweight championship.

Ali began to plan the path that would regain him his title, but he was so spent from the Frazier bout that he really should have rested. Unfortunately, his manager Herbert Muhammad and promoter Bob Arum had cooked up a money-making scheme that needed to be tended to. Prior to the loss to Frazier, the two had agreed to pit Ali against the behemoth basketball star, Wilt Chamberlain, who at 7'2" and 275 pounds would have been imposing indeed. The gate, they thought, would be enormous. Not surprisingly, the strange bout never took place. Chamberlain's entourage claimed that the reason involved ancillary financial rights that Ali's people wouldn't grant. Arum told a different story. At the signing, as soon as Chamberlain entered the room, Ali screamed, "Timber," an obvious jab at his height and likelihood of falling in the ring. At that point, according to Arum, "Chamberlain turns white, goes into the room with his lawyer, comes out, and says he's not fighting" (Hauser 237). Whatever really happened, Ali was free to rest up for the first leg of his journey back: a July bout against former sparring partner Jimmy Ellis for the vacant North American Boxing Association title.

The Ellis fight was the first in a series of bouts all designed to prepare Ali for a Frazier rematch. It would be a bittersweet contest. Ellis was not only a former sparring partner but a boyhood friend. With Ali's consent, Angelo Dundee, who trained both fighters, was in Ellis's corner, but even his experience couldn't overcome Ali's skill. He knocked out Ellis with a powerful right hand in the 12th round even though Ellis said he had been looking for the punch and knew it was coming.

During the next six months, Ali fought 11 bouts, nine exhibitions, and two full-fledged contests, against his friend Buster Mathis and German Jurgen Blin, winning by a decision against Mathis and knocking out Blin in the 7th round. Ali was criticized for being too compassionate in the Mathis bout by some of the same journalists who attacked him for torturing Ernie Terrell and Floyd Patterson in previous contests. Interestingly, after the fight, Mathis went to Ali's dressing room in tears of gratitude and thanked the champ "for the opportunity to make money" and for the "honor" of fighting him (Hauser 242).

Frazier spent most of 1971 and all of 1972 avoiding his nemesis, fighting only a few exhibitions and two championship bouts, both of which the referee stopped in the 4th round. Frazier explained his relative lack of activity as a response to potential tax problems if he made too much money. But his refusal to fight Ali had much more to do with his reaction to some of Ali's comments in the weeks following their initial bout. In his autobiography, Frazier extensively and angrily quotes one of "Clay's" diatribes against him:

> Joe Frazier is ugly, he don't talk good, he's got no footwork. All he does is take punches. He's not recognized when he walks the streets.... In Japan they treated me like a president. All the things I stand for, all the things I went through... being a Muslim, staying out of the Army, being deprived of my right to work for almost four years... and to go fifteen hard rounds and send him to the hospital is why people still regard me as the champion. HE says he's satisfied. Sure he's satisfied, with a crumb. Man been in a meathouse all his life, he's thankful to get a crumb. White folks... give a nigger a crumb and expect him to be thankful (Frazier 124).

Of course, this was Ali at his adolescent macho best—or worst. Perhaps he believed what he said. Or maybe he was shrewdly trying to build a gate for the fight to come (doubtful given the fact that interest in a rematch was already huge). More likely, he was still smarting from the defeat. Whatever the reasons, his outburst hurt and angered Joe. He decided that Ali was simply a sore loser. And the more he pondered, the madder he got: "[E]very time Clay opened his big mouth, it made me want to keep his ass on hold" (Frazier 130).

Meanwhile, Ali kept up a remarkable schedule of exhibitions and North American Boxing Federation (NABF) title fights in 1972. In that one year he fought 26 exhibitions, four title fights, and two nontitle bouts. Amazingly, he boxed in major fights three times in three months, defeating Mac Foster in 15 rounds in Tokyo in April and defending his title against George Chuvalo in May and Jerry Quarry in June. He then gave Floyd Patterson a rematch in September. Interestingly, Howard Cosell remembers being very concerned about the Patterson fight. Ali signed the papers at the same time he was doing color commentary with Cosell at the 1972 Olympic boxing matches. Cosell warned his friend: "I don't want you to hurt him," no doubt recalling the punishment Ali lavished on Patterson in their previous bout. Ali told Cosell that he had no intention of hurting Patterson. In fact, Ali said that the bout was an act of kindness. Patterson was having tax problems—a fact that Cosell confirmed later—and Ali agreed to the fight to provide Patterson a payday (Cosell 239). Ali won the bout with a 7th round knockout. He then fought lightweight champion Bob Foster in November after a scheduled bout in South Africa against Al Jones had been cancelled. Outweighed by 41 pounds, Foster went down for the count in the 8th round.[11]

And still no Frazier. In fact, Frazier's manager, Yank Durham, decided that his fighter should take on a rising young heavyweight, George Foreman, in Kingston, Jamaica, on January 22, 1973. Foreman, born in 1949 and raised in a tough Houston ghetto, had an impressive career. After losing his first amateur fight in August 1968 (by disqualification), he captured the Olympic heavyweight championship that year in Mexico City. Many Americans were thrilled when after winning the final bout, he ran around the ring, waiving a small U.S. flag, in clear contrast to medal winning track stars Tommie Smith and John Carlos, who gave a black power salute when the American National Anthem was played. Foreman turned pro in 1969 and by the time he was to meet Frazier, had rattled off 37 straight victories, all but three by knockout. Nonetheless, Frazier was unimpressed. He concluded that Foreman's record was based on "[beating] up mostly tomato cans," not the kind of "recognized tough guys" that he had faced early in his career. A confident Frazier, however, ran into a powerhouse that night. Frazier went down three times in the 1st round and three more times in the second, when the referee mercifully stopped the fight. Frazier was stunned—"left with a hollow feeling," as he found himself "just a contender" (Frazier 131, 135).

Ali must have felt hollow as well. Frazier's defeat meant that the next Ali–Frazier bout had lost much of its luster. But Ali kept fighting, with the possibility of a Foreman bout in mind. After the Bob Foster bout, Ali took on Joe Bugner in Las Vegas, who actually lasted the full 12 rounds.[12] Ali hoped that his next bout, against Ken Norton, would propel him into a championship match against Foreman.

Norton was 29–1 when he faced Ali on March 31, 1973, but most of his opponents were hardly giants in the field. In fact, the purse at Norton's most recent bout prior to the Ali fight had been only $300, and it had been fought before a paltry 700 spectators. Ali's people took Norton so lightly that they didn't even arrange for a closed-circuit broadcast of the contest. But Norton had been Frazier's sparring partner. And one of Frazier's corner men, Eddie Futch, prepared Norton well. In the 2nd round, Norton caught Ali flush in the jaw and broke it. Ferdie Pacheco says he wanted to stop the fight, but Ali and manager Herbert Muhammad wanted the fight to go on, fearing that a technical knockout would hurt Ali's image, especially among blacks who might be potential converts. Ferdie sadly admits that he also should have thrown in the towel then but was concerned "about the criticism and ire it would raise with the black establishment if a white doctor… stopped the fight against Ali's and Herbert's wishes" (Pacheco 114). Ali went the full 12 rounds. Indeed, he might have won had Norton not clearly taken the final round. Norton earned a unanimous decision. After the fight, the doctor who performed surgery on Ali's jaw mused, "I can't fathom how he could go on the whole fight like that" (Hauser 253).

For many, the stunning loss to Norton, no matter how much courage Ali displayed, marked the beginning of the end of his career. Sportswriter Jimmy Cannon, who never much cared for Ali, concluded that he was "a loser now," in fact, "an old loser." Even his good friend Howard Cosell thought at the time that "losing to Norton was the end of the road" (Hauser 252). But as so often would happen in his career, like the Phoenix rising from the ashes, Ali came back. After six months of recuperation, he fought Norton again. Norton's awkward style still befuddled Ali so that he needed a strong final round to eke out a close but unanimous decision. This victory set the stage for the second Ali–Frazier bout, again at Madison Square Garden.

The two fighters engaged in even more vitriolic verbal sparring than before the first bout. Frazier said that as he went back to training, "back to the bullshit went Clay" (Frazier 143). Ali kept playing on the "Frazier as stupid" motif. At one point he said that Frazier was ignorant for wanting to bring up his son to be a prizefighter: "Me, I'm gonna make my son a lawyer or a doctor.... My daughter is four.... She says, 'I want to be a doctor'" (Hauser 255).[13] At a news conference that announced the fight, Ali called Frazier an Uncle Tom, to which a furious Frazier responded, "My skin is blacker than yours. Maybe you're really a half-breed" (Frazier 143). Ali made a move toward Frazier but was restrained. A few weeks later, the two actually did tangle physically while being interviewed about their first fight by Howard Cosell on ABC's *Wide World of Sports*. When Frazier commented on Ali's swollen jaw after the bout, Ali made a reference to Frazier's long stay in the hospital. They traded insults, then Ali's brother, Rudy, leaped on stage, Ali grabbed Joe, as if in a bear hug, and Frazier threw him to the ground where they rolled around until separated. After leaving the studio, Frazier was convinced that standing up to Ali would get inside his head: "Did you see how wide that nigger's eyes opened up. Now I really got him scared" (Hauser 257).[14]

If Ali was frightened, he didn't show it in the fight. Madison Square Garden was packed again and filled with celebrities, including John Kennedy Jr. and his sister Caroline, as well as George Foreman. The bout went 12 rounds—with far less punishment dished out by the two than in the first bout. Ali basically held off Frazier, with some 133 clinches, while flicking enough jabs to garner a unanimous decision. He did rock Frazier in the 2nd round, but referee Tony Perez mistakenly thought the round was over and separated the fighters. Frazier was convinced that he had been robbed. He and his corner believed that Ali had illegally grabbed Joe's head and pulled it down during the fight. He pointed out that Red Smith and Dave Anderson of the *New York Times* thought Frazier had won. In fact Anderson wondered if the referee and judges had been influenced by Ali's constant complaining about the outcome of the initial bout. Frazier believed that "Clay got a gift from the judges" and that he and they were simply "victims of Clay's popularity" (Frazier 148). Perhaps forgetting that he had waited 35 months before agreeing to fight Ali a second time, Frazier demanded a rematch. This time, however, he would have to wait. Ali had bigger fish to fry in Zaire.

Frazier was right about one thing. Between 1970 and 1974, Muhammad Ali had become, if not a hero, immensely popular and acknowledged to be a superb heavyweight prizefighter. Events worked in Ali's favor. The Supreme Court overturned, with little negative public reaction, his conviction for refusing induction into the military. Military participation in the Vietnam War ended with a cease-fire agreement in January 1973 shortly before Ali, clad in Elvis's cloak, had beaten Joe Bugner. By the time he defeated Frazier, the Nixon Administration was in a freefall because of the Watergate scandal. Thus, many of the forces that had coalesced to demonize Ali had dissipated. And Ali had softened as well. To be sure, he continued to bad mouth many of his opponents, especially Joe Frazier. But, as we have seen, he signed to give Floyd Patterson a rematch to help alleviate his financial problems. And once freed of his legal burden by the Supreme Court, Ali refused to criticize the prosecutors, juries, and judges that had sought to put him in jail.

Three very telling anecdotes are suggestive of this growing change in Ali. While training at Deer Lake, Pennsylvania, for the second Patterson fight, he visited a nursing home where an elderly man thought Ali was Joe Louis. He looked at him ecstatically and said, "All my life I've wanted to meet you, Joe." Ali simply replied, "That's right. I'm Joe Louis," then hugged the man and said, "God Bless you." Pretending to be Louis for the sake of an old man was an especially poignant gesture, given the highly ambiguous relationship between the two great heavyweights.

When Ali was training for a bout with George Foreman, a father whose son, Jimmy, was dying of leukemia asked Ali if he could visit his son. Ali invited them both to the training camp and spent most of the day talking to the boy, joking and hamming it up. The child's father admitted that he had hated Ali throughout his career and hoped that he would lose his fights. He realized, however, that Ali was "a good man" and admitted that he was "sorry for the way I felt about him" (Hauser 247). Later, Ali went to visit Jimmy in the hospital. Ali tried to cheer him up by saying the he would beat Foreman and Jimmy would beat cancer. The boy responded, "No, Muhammad, I'm going to meet God, and I'm going to tell Him that you are my friend." Ali found out that at Jimmy's funeral, there was a photograph of him in the coffin next to the young boy's head (Ali, *Butterfly* 122, 123).

Finally, one day some children with cerebral palsy visited Ali's camp. Ralph Thornton, who joined Ali's retinue at Deer Lake, recalls that they all slobbered badly. Without hesitating, Ali leaned down and kissed each one "dead on the mouth, slobber all over him.... You could see how much they loved him" (Hauser 247, 248).

The two Alis—the blustering braggart who attacked opponents, often insulting their intelligence and, if black, their commitment to their race and the child-like lover of people, especially children—would appear together in November 1974 when Muhammad Ali accomplished what virtually no one thought he could. He regained the heavyweight title against George Foreman, one of the most formidable fighters in the history of the sport.

NOTES

1. Paterno also said that although he probably would have gone to Vietnam if drafted, he understood why principled other people might refuse. He ultimately concluded in the early 1970s that "the war was very wrong" (Hauser 200).

2. Ali, of course, was aware of Maddox's fury. At one point when he was training for the bout at his old haunt, the 5th Street Gym in Miami, he learned that Maddox had declared a day of mourning because of the fight. Ali quipped, "My, my, [the fight will happen] right under the nose of Lester Maddox himself. Ain't the world strange. The Lord must have a lot of fun, don't he?" (Kram 101).

3. Although Sylvester Stallone denies it, Joe likes to think this his battles with the beef gave Stallone the idea for a similar scene in *Rocky I*.

4. Frazier also jawboned a number of former greats such as Jack Dempsey at a boxing dinner one night. He recalls going "around the table like the last supper," trying to convince yesterday's heroes to speak out for Ali's restoration (Brunt 116). There is no evidence that any of Frazier's efforts had any impact on the final decision to restore the license in Atlanta and New York.

5. Ali called Frazier the night before the fight for a little last minute bantering: "You sure you're not scared, Joe Frazier?" To which Joe gave as good as he got: "[Just] scared of what I'm going to do to you," he replied. He ended the conversation warning Ali not to be late (Kram 139).

6. This was a regular ritual in prizefighting, insurance against a boxer doctoring his gloves with illegal chemicals or stuffing them with heavy objects. One of Ali's people would have been in Frazier's dressing room as well.

7. Both fighters wound up in hospitals after the bout. After x-rays of his swollen jaw proved negative for breaks, Ali didn't want to stay overnight for fear that people would think that Frazier had hurt him seriously. Frazier, in worse shape than his opponent, didn't want to go to the hospital at all. He thought if Ali found out he would "make more headlines, show how he beat me so bad I gotta be put in a hospital." He felt so weak, however, that he surreptitiously went to a hometown hospital in Philadelphia, where he became dangerously ill with high blood pressure and a kidney infection. At one point in his delirium he pleaded with Joe Hand, a police officer who guarded him, "Don't let Ali find out that I'm here" (Kram 148). According to the doctors who attended him, Frazier almost died.

8. Some of this stoicism must have been one of Ali's masks. When he ended the press conference with "You lose, you don't kill yourself," a reporter interrupted, informing Ali that Frazier had said he didn't think Ali wanted to fight him again. Ali fumed, "Oh, how wrong he is" (Hauser 233).

9. Neither Frazier nor Smith gloated as much as Frazier's brother, Tom. As a defeated Ali left the ring, Tom, "tears in his eyes, screamed at him 'Crawl. Crawl on your knees to Joe Frazier'" (Kram 147).

10. Chief Justice Warren Burger was profoundly upset by the decision and was inclined to dissent. According to journalist Bob Woodward, Burger decided to concur, finally, because otherwise "it might be interpreted as a racist vote." He hoped that a unanimous decision "would be a good lift for black people" (Woodward and Armstrong, *The Brethren* 138).

11. Foster recalls that because the fight was organized on such short notice, the only venue available was a nightclub: "You go up to the ring, and there are people sitting there, eating dinner, having drinks all around you." Foster must have imbibed a bit himself that night because he bragged that he "had hurt Ali early" with his jabs. Foster also claimed he had "the hardest jab in boxing," which must have been news to Ali, although he did open a cut above Ali's eye. Foster even thought he could have won if Ali's weight advantage hadn't worn him down (Hauser 250).

12. Ali might have been distracted by the fact that one of his heroes, Elvis Presley, gave him a "white bejeweled robe bearing the legend 'People's Champion,'" which he felt obligated to wear into the ring. As Thomas Hauser notes, "Fashion experts, such as they are in boxing, observed that the attire was somewhat gaudy" (Hauser 250).

13. Ali's comment is an interesting revision of the more traditional view of the American dream that he fulfilled through fighting. Similar to so many Americans, he wanted a better life for his children, but through more "respectable" professions. He poignantly noted, "Me, I'm not educated so good, but I have enough money and enough sense to know how important education is" (Hauser 255).

14. The New York State Athletic Committee fined each fighter $5,000 for the altercation—the largest fines in the commission's history.

Chapter 8

FROM FOREMAN TO RETIREMENT: THE LAST PROFESSIONAL YEARS

The heavyweight championship fight between Muhammad Ali and George Foreman would probably not have taken place without the efforts of two very different black men who, at the time, had common goals. Don King, a young promoter who had wandered around the edges of professional fighting for several years, convinced Ali and Foreman to sign. But the large guarantee he needed was supplied by Mobutu Sese Seko, the President of Zaire (formerly the Belgian Congo). Mobutu not only guaranteed a $10 million purse to be split by the two fighters but he also invested heavily in a venue in which to stage the bout and the technology needed to broadcast the fight on radio and closed-circuit television. He hoped that the publicity generated by the extravaganza would boost the image of his country and, no doubt, himself throughout the world. The two fighters were eager to participate.[1]

The fight would be the first ever heavyweight championship contest staged in Africa—a fitting venue for a battle between two powerful African Americans. Originally scheduled for September 25, 1974, the bout was postponed for five weeks when Foreman suffered a serious injury while sparring only eight days prior to the bout. Members of both camps assumed that the parties would leave Africa and return shortly before the rescheduled fight. But Mobutu's chief advisor would not allow them to depart, fearing that they might not come back to fight.

The enforced stay probably bothered Foreman and his people more than it did Ali. Foreman tended to be reclusive, staying in the fancy Westernized Intercontinental Hotel in downtown Kinshasa, the capital city where the fight would take place. Ali, on the other hand, loved to spend time mingling with the local citizens. According to Bobby Goodman, who worked publicity in Ali's camp, "Almost from the beginning, Ali was embraced by the people in Zaire," in part because he "had a reputation that he was a man fighting for his people" (Cassidy 91). The atmosphere absolutely energized Ali.

Few people, however, except perhaps Ali and most of the thousands of Zaireans who enthusiastically cheered for him, believed that he had a chance to regain the heavyweight championship title against Foreman. After all, the champ was younger, heavier, and undefeated. In fact, Foreman had won 40 consecutive professional fights, 37 by knockouts. Most worrying to Ali's camp was the fact two of those knockouts came against Joe Frazier and Ken Norton before the end of the second round, two fighters to whom Ali had lost. According to many who followed the fight game, Foreman, in the words of sportswriter Dave Anderson, "might be the heaviest puncher in the history of the heavyweight division." Foreman agreed: "My opponents don't worry about losing. They worry about getting hurt" (Hauser 260).

But even though the *New York Times* in banner headlines trumpeted the fact that bookies had Foreman at 3-1 odds to defeat Ali, the 32-year old former champion and self-proclaimed "King of the World" showed supreme confidence (*New York Times*, 29 October 1974, 45). In customary style, Ali openly taunted his opponent; part cocky adolescent, part clown. "George Foreman is nothing but a big mummy. [He] hits hard but hitting power don't mean nothing if you can't find nothing to hit. George Foreman don't stand a chance." He actually advised fans watching on closed-circuit television "to get to their theaters and don't be late, because I might end it in one round" (Hauser 266, 267, 271). Ali even claimed to have developed a special new punch for the fight. According to journalist Robert Cassidy, he dubbed it "The Ghetto Whopper" since it was the very blow "that was thrown in the ghetto at three o'clock in the morning" (Cassidy 91).[2]

The day before the fight, both fighters attended a garden party hosted by Zaire's president, Mobutu Sese Seko. On the evening of the fight, Ali watched a horror film, slept for a few hours, then joined his bulging entourage for the bus ride to the national soccer stadium where 60,000 fans awaited, most of them African, most of them fiercely loyal to Ali, and a few even fearing an early departure by their hero.

Ali's dressing room was crowded with unofficial members of his camp as well as trainer Angelo Dundee, doctor Ferdie Pacheco, resident clown and so-called assistant trainer Bundini Brown, manager Herbert Muhammad, Ali's brother Rudy, and assorted others including "a small fat

Turk named Hassan," as well as journalists Norman Mailer and George Plimpton (Mailer 164). Virtually everyone was somber except Ali. Mailer told the challenger that he "was more scared than you are," to which Ali blithely replied, "'Nothing to be scared about. It's just another day in the dramatic life of Muhammad Ali.... We're going to dance. We're going to dance."

According to boxing tradition, Ali, as challenger, would be the first to enter the ring. Shortly before 4:00 A.M. he donned the white African robe he had decided to wear, no doubt in honor of the venue and his thousands of African fans. Then he and 19 of his retinue, raced down the long concrete hall from the dressing room to the stadium, led by a platoon of Zairean soldiers. As Ali entered, a roar went up from his fans, most of them seated far from the action. A temporary tin roof had been constructed over part of the outdoor stadium to protect the fighters and the 2,500 occupants of pricey ringside seats from the predicted rainstorm. Foreman arrived in the ring 10 minutes after Ali, wearing red trunks with a white stripe and a blue waistband—a walking American flag. One of his corner men, former light heavyweight champion Archie Moore, recalls that just prior to the fight he "was praying, and in great sincerity, that George wouldn't *kill* Ali. I really felt that was a possibility" (Mailer 176).

If Ali was worried that these might be his final moments, he certainly didn't show fear before the opening bell. He mocked Foreman during the playing of the national anthems; when Foreman was putting on his gloves, according to sportswriter Dave Anderson, Ali "swooped near him and taunted him with a mock look, to the delight of the crowd" (Anderson 55). He even taunted Foreman during the referee's instructions: "Chump, you're gonna get yourself beat tonight in front of all these Africans. I'm gonna hit you everywhere but under the bottom of your big funky feet" (Ali, *Greatest* 403).

Ali's trainer and corner men also weren't concerned about his demise. Indeed, they just assumed that their fighter would dance the champ silly, using speed to wear out the more ponderous Foreman, and above all, avoid getting hit excessively. Angelo Dundee was convinced that his fighter would win by following this strategy. But Ali realized that heat and humidity had caused the floor of the ring to become soft, or "slow" in boxing lingo. He also noticed during the first round that Foreman was skilled in cutting off the ring and Ali's ability to maneuver; thus excessive dancing and darting would have caused his legs to tire. Ali then improvised a remarkable plan. After delivering a thumping blow to Foreman's head at the outset of the opening round—"No opponent had cracked

George this hard in years," Norman Mailer observed—in the middle of round two, Ali retreated to the ropes and simply let Foreman flail away (Mailer 178). Thus he had created on the spur of the moment what he later called the "rope-a-dope" tactic.

His corner was apoplectic at what they saw as a strategy that would surely lead to defeat. As Angelo Dundee recalls, "When he went to the ropes, I felt sick" (Hauser 276). Bundini Brown and others screamed at their fighter to get off the ropes. But Ali knew what he was doing. To be sure, as he admits, Foreman hurt him badly with some of this fearsome right hand shots, but Ali also saw that as the bout went on, Foreman's blows landed with decreasing force and mainly on elbows and upper arms. Moreover, the challenger began to rag the champ: "Hit harder! Show me something George. That don't hurt. I thought you were supposed to be bad" (Hauser 277). Ali even got the crowd to practice a bit of psychological warfare. Between rounds and occasionally during the fight, he would wave his arms, encouraging them to cheer and scream the refrain he had heard from his African fans since he arrived: "Ali, bomaye"—"Ali, kill him."

In the third round Ali mainly lay against the ropes. Although he absorbed some wicked punches, he didn't even sit in his corner at the end of the round. Rather he ambled over to the ringside television cameras and mugged one of his patented silly expressions. He continued to spend most of his time on the ropes for the next four rounds, usually bouncing off them for a few well-placed jabs to Foreman's face as each round ended.

Foreman, stumbling and tired, chased Ali during the 7th round, but he was clearly hurt. His face was puffy, particularly the right eye, which he had injured earlier while sparring in his camp. By the 8th round, it was clear that Foreman was exhausted. Near the end of the round, with Foreman stumbling backwards, Ali delivered a devastating left-right combination, with the chopping right hand sending Foreman to the mat. With Ali shuffling in his corner, referee Zack Clayton counted out the champion with two seconds remaining in the round.

The crowd exploded, as dozens of Ali supporters burst through military lines to descend on the new champion. Ali seemed almost dazed; in fact, he sat down in the middle of the ring for several seconds. Norman Mailer thought he had fainted, perhaps from "a private bolt from Allah," Mailer speculated, "a warning against excessive pride" (Mailer 210). Ali recalls that he just wanted to get to his dressing room. There, according to Mailer, he "stared out like a child," looking like a happy and tired host after a good party: "I have stolen the jam," his eyes said, "and it tastes good." Ali thought that "maybe they'll admit that now I am the professor of boxing" (Mailer 212).

Initially, Foreman was devastated. He hinted darkly at various conspiracies—including nefariously loosened ring ropes, a quick count by the referee, even drugged water—to account for his stunning defeat. But on reflection, he concluded, "I was drugged alright. Muhammad gave me a dose of that big right hand" (Hauser 278). Or as he confessed to author Stephen Brunt a quarter century after the fight: "Muhammad Ali whipped me" (Brunt 189).

As for Ali, he and his retinue headed back to his compound just outside Kinshasa during the driving rainstorm that had been predicted earlier. Ferdie Pacheco remembers the trip: "It was like the return of a victorious army. All through the jungle, people were lined up along the road with children in their arms, waiting for Ali in the pouring rain" (Hauser 279).[3] The entourage celebrated for a while, then broke up as dawn was breaking, leaving Ali on the stoop of his cottage. *Newsweek* reporter Pete Bonventre, who had been delayed by the storm, arrived in time to witness a remarkable scene: Ali was on his stoop showing a magic trick to a group of delighted African kids. Bonventre observed that "it was hard to tell who was having a better time, Ali or the children." Thus Ali, who had been the man who had scored a great upset only three hours earlier, only the second fighter in history to regain the heavyweight championship, was still a child on that wet African morning. Bonventre concluded, "There'll never be anyone like him again" (Hauser 279).

Muhammad Ali was on an incredible high after he defeated George Foreman against all odds and most prognostications. Part of his joy was no doubt related to the fact that he made a lot of money for slightly less than 24 minutes of boxing. His $5,450,000 gross share was more than Joe Louis, Jack Dempsey, or Rocky Marciano made in their entire careers. But he also evened the score with the observers of boxing who questioned his ability to win. Immediately after the bout, British commentator David Frost tried to interview the new and resurgent champion. In typical form, Ali commandeered the interview and scolded those who still doubted him (in the press). According to Robert Cassidy, Ali exclaimed, "Everybody stop talking right now. Attention." Then he

> focused his gaze directly at the camera. His right eye was lightly swollen and discolored. He pointed his right index finger at the camera and began to lecture:
> "I told you, all of my critics, I told you that I was the greatest of all time when I beat Sonny Liston. I told you today I'm still the

greatest of all time.... Never again say that I'm going to be defeated. Never again make me the underdog until I'm about 50 years old. Then you might get me." (Cassidy 97)

Perhaps even more remarkable was the fact that President Gerald Ford sought to honor Ali by inviting him to the White House a few weeks after the Foreman bout. Such an invitation was simply not thinkable during the Johnson and Nixon administrations, when Clay/Ali was a pariah, not a national hero. But times had changed with the end of the Vietnam War. Besides, President Ford, a former college football player himself, was a great fan of boxing, and, as he told Thomas Hauser, he "wanted to meet Muhammad... because it was part of my overall effort to heal the wounds of racial division, Vietnam, and Watergate." He said he thoroughly enjoyed a chat with a man "who never lacked words" and who was "a man of principle." The President concluded, with some prescience, "I'm quite sure that his page [in history] will talk about him as more than just a superb athlete" (Hauser 281, 282).

A number of observers didn't wait until history had a chance to talk. *Ring Magazine*, which had failed to designate a fighter of the year in 1966 so as not to have to honor Ali, gave him that title for 1974. *Sports Illustrated* named him Sportsman of the Year, and he was awarded the Hickok Belt as the outstanding amateur athlete in 1974. Journalist Maury Allen best summed up the swelling chorus of praise in the months after the Foreman fight: "It is time to recognize Ali for what he is; the greatest athlete of his time and maybe all time and one of the most important and brave men of all American time" (Hauser 281).

But there were downs as well as ups in the days after the fight. His marriage to Belinda was under increasing strain mainly because of his roving eye. Ali admitted that he liked to pursue the ladies, but he tried to rationalize his penchant: "If I got a girl friend on the side, it's nobody's business but mine. There are many pretty girls in my camp.... But what I do behind locked doors is my private affair" (Hano 119). One of those ladies was Veronica Porsche, a Creole beauty who was one of four poster girls chosen to publicize the Foreman bout and who accompanied promoter Don King to Africa. Ali was smitten when he first saw her and squired her around Zaire even though his wife was present. One time Belinda actually caught them returning to the hotel at 1:00 A. M. She confessed, "I smacked him good; scratched him a bit. I would have whupped Veronica worse, but she ran and I didn't know who she was" (Hauser 311). Husband and wife reached an uneasy truce after returning to the United States, although Ali continued to see Veronica.

Adding to Ali's problems was the death of Elijah Muhammad on February 25, 1975. He recalls that the death made him extremely said. After all, Elijah had been like a spiritual father to the young fighter. Nonetheless, in spite of his grief, he realized that Elijah had his flaws. And when the NOI split into factions after his death, Ali followed Elijah's son, Wallace, who "changed the direction of the Nation" in ways of which the champ approved. Ali shared Wallace's views on race and religion: "He's learned from his studies that his father wasn't teaching true Islam, and Wallace taught us the true meaning of the Qur'an. He showed that color don't matter" (Hauser 294). Interestingly, this view echoed that of Malcolm X a decade earlier when he split with Elijah.

But neither domestic troubles nor religious questions deflected Ali from his central focus: he wanted to fight and defend his crown, ultimately in the rubber match against Joe Frazier. On the path to Frazier, Ali successfully defended his title three times: against an especially courageous Chuck Wepner as well as Ron Lyle and Joe Bugner. Although he scored no early knockouts, he won the fights convincingly (save for the one against Lyle, in which he was lackadaisical until pounding out an 11th-round knockout). The Wepner fight contained two interesting sidelights. Ali bad-mouthed referee Tony Perez after the bout because he thought the referee had allowed Wepner to use illegal tactics. Ali said that Perez was "a dirty dog" who was "neither black nor white, but Puerto Rican." Perez sued, lost the case, then reconciled when Ali told him he loved him and gave him a big kiss after the trial (Hauser 299, 300). And in a moment fraught with meaning for American pop culture, an out-of-work actor named Sylvester Stallone coughed up $20 to see the fight on closed-circuit television and was awed by Wepner's gutsy performance—he lasted until a 15th-round TKO. Stallone used this inspiration to write a screenplay he titled *Rocky*, the movie that launched his career.

Ali's next title defense would be the final chapter in one of the great sports rivalries as he took on Joe Frazier in Manila, the capital of the Philippines. President Ferdinand Marcos, like Mobutu in Zaire, offered to bankroll the fight because of the spotlight it would shine on his country. Obviously, it would be a huge money maker and attention grabber. But in the run-up to the fight, Ali's personal life exploded in the media. He had brought his mistress, Veronica, to the bout and introduced her to President Marcos, which left the impression that she was the boxer's wife. When the story broke, Belinda flew to Manila, stormed into Ali's hotel room, and began throwing furniture. She stormed back out, with a parting shout to her husband: "You tell that bitch that, if I see her I'm going to break her back" (Hauser 319). Belinda got on the same plane she arrived in and flew back to the United States.

For a few moments it looked as if the Ali–Ali fight would be more newsworthy and vicious than the Ali–Frazier fight. But the champ got things back on track, partly because of his continued taunting of Frazier. Previously, back in the United States at the press conference that announced the fight, he had chanted, "It's gonna be a thilla and a chilla and a killa when I get the gorilla in Manila." And to confirm the Frazier-simian ape comparison, the champ pulled a small rubber gorilla from his pocket, showed it to Frazier, claiming he would keep the beast tucked in his breast pocket at all times. Frazier responded feebly, "It's kind of nice to know that [soon]...I'll be the champ again" (Cassidy 98, 99). Ali also kept up the drumbeat in remarks at his training camp in Pennsylvania. He and Bundini Brown had perfected a taunting call and response. When a spectator claimed that Frazier was the greatest, an angry Ali screamed, "Joe Frazier should give his face to the Wildlife Fund. He so ugly, blind men go the other way." To which, Bundini "slapped his thighs and replied, "Ugly, ugly, ugly" (Kram 169). In his own training camp, Frazier was dead serious. He told Eddie Futch not to stop the fight no matter how hurt he seemed: "We got nowhere to go after this. I'm gonna eat this half-breed's heart right out of his chest." It would be a fight, perhaps, to the death: "This is the end of him or me," Frazier concluded (Kram 171).

Ali repeated the gorilla motif as often as he could after the two fighters and their entourages arrived in the Philippines, with his staccato mantra: "Come on gorilla, we in Manila,...this is a thrilla" (Cassidy 99). Frazier, unsurprisingly, was livid at the implications of the gorilla label: "I hated that man," he told Thomas Hauser. "First two fights, he tried to make me a white man. Then he tried to make me a nigger. How would you like it if your kids came home from school crying, because everyone was calling their daddy a gorilla?"(Hauser 325).

The verbiage certainly didn't sap Joe of any of his determination. The fight took place on October 1, 1975, with Ali a 2–1 favorite. Ali recalls praying with Herbert Muhammad before the bout, seeing himself as a crucial symbol to millions of Muslims throughout the world. And even though the fight was scheduled for 10:30 P.M. so as to accommodate closed-circuit television venues in the United States, Angelo Dundee believed that it was hotter than in Zaire, especially because a tin roof helped keep the heat and humidity locked in the enclosed space.

The fight ebbed and flowed. Ali was the aggressor for the first few rounds, seemingly trying to end the fight early. But when he took to the ropes in the 5th round, Frazier went after him. Frazier jarred the champ with a massive left hook in the 6th round. Ed Schuyler of the Associated Press claimed it was even harder than the one Frazier landed in their first bout. But this time Ali stayed up, looked at Frazier and said, "They told me Joe Frazier was washed up." Frazier responded, "They lied" (Hauser 321). They kept hammering each other, neither man backing down, through heat and humidity. Gradually, the champ began to wear down Frazier, who was bleeding from the mouth and was barely able to open his eyes. At the end of the 14th round, even though he seemed to be winning, Ali was so exhausted that he asked his trainer to cut off his gloves and stop the fight. At the same time Dundee was trying to talk Ali out of quitting, Eddie Futch, Frazier's chief corner man, decided that Frazier, who could no longer see out of his battered eyes, was done. He threw in the towel. Frazier pleaded, "No, no, no! You can't do that to me." But Futch replied, perhaps recalling fighters he had seen seriously injured, even killed in the ring, "Sit down, son. It's over. No one will ever forget what you did here today" (Kram 187). One of the greatest fights in history was over. Muhammad Ali had won the series and defended his title.

In the aftermath, both fighters experienced a deeply painful exhaustion. Frazier was in tears as he lay on a couch in his dressing room: "Man, I hit him with punches that bring down the walls of a city. What held him up?" For Ali there was a grisly footnote to the bout. A policeman stationed in his dressing room had accidentally blown half his head off while twirling his pistol. His body lay on the floor, blood splattered on the mirror, as Ali screamed, "A dead man! Get me out of here" (Kram 188). Ali's people found another room and a couch, on which he collapsed. Later that night he could barely eat his food as guest of honor in the presidential palace, with his face raw, his right eye almost shut, his skin full of splotches. The next day, he was still urinating blood from the blows he had taken. He complained, "Everything in me is on flame." He reflected on the fight, deciding that he was lucky not to have been killed by the punches Frazier landed. "I must be crazy," he concluded. "This is it for me. It's over" (Kram 189).

Of course it wasn't over. Perhaps he should have retired with this remarkable triumph. We can plausibly argue that it was the pinnacle of his career, that in spite of future victories and comebacks, in a sense, his career and impact were never quite the same as the 1970s limped toward their end, with the United States out of Vietnam, inflation growing rapidly, and American hostages taken in Iran. But Ali did keep fighting—10 more times throughout the next six years.

Ali settled one score with Ken Norton in September 1976. They had each won a hard earned victory, with Norton one of only two men to defeat the champ. The third fight was a reprise of the first two. Norton led early, then Ali made a comeback, so that, again, all depended on the last round. Norton coasted until the final thirty seconds, but Ali had scored enough points to win a close but unanimous decision. Referee Arthur Mercante noted that Ali was simply "not the same fighter" he had been against Frazier in their first bout. "His timing was off; he tired more easily" (Hauser 339). Nonetheless, he had enough boxing savvy to win.[4]

But Ali's personal life was in turmoil again. His parents had separated, mainly because of Cassius Sr.'s philandering. Ali bought his mother, Odessa, a home, and she left her husband. Of course, Ali had been cheating on his wife Belinda for years. She simply could not take sharing him with Veronica Porsche any more and filed for divorce shortly before the Norton fight. In 1977, after the divorce was finalized, Ali married Veronica.

In his next bout, in May 1977, he faced a young Spaniard, Alfredo Evangelista, who had been a professional boxer for only 19 months. Perhaps still fretting about marital problems, Ali was uninspiring to say the least. The bout lasted for 15 boring rounds, with Ali garnering a decision. According to Howard Cosell, "It was one of the worst fights ever fought" (Hauser 341). His next defense, against Ernie Shavers, was a struggle. Although Ali was leading after 12 rounds, Shavers was coming on strong and rocked the champ in the 14th round. Journalist Pat Putnam was convinced that Ali was done after that round: "When the bell for the fifteenth round rang, Ali could barely stand." Putnam believed that the final round of that fight showed Ali's clear boxing genius, even though he was "long past his prime" (Hauser 346). Sheer willpower kept him on his feet.

Ali's ring doctor, Pacheco, came to the conclusion after the Shavers fight that willpower would not be enough to save Ali from potential permanent damage. The day after the fight, a New York State Athletic Commission physician told Pacheco that Ali's prefight lab results revealed potentially severe kidney damage as well as neurological deterioration. Pacheco was so concerned that he sent letters to Ali, his wife, manager Herbert Muhammad, trainer Angelo Dundee, and NOI head Wallace Muhammad, urging that Ali retire from the ring. When he received no responses, he decided to leave: "If a national treasure like Ali could not be saved, at least I didn't have to be a part of his undoing" (Pacheco 151).

Muhammad Ali continued to fight. Promoter Butch Lewis wanted him to take on one of his prospects, Leon Spinks. Ali adamantly refused because Leon had only five professional bouts under his belt at the time.[5]

But the champ changed his mind when he realized an Ali–Spinks contest would have an interesting hook. Spinks had won an Olympic gold medal in boxing in 1976. When he realized this, Ali excitedly told Lewis that he had beaten three other gold medal winners—Patterson, Foreman, and Frazier—and wanted to add a fourth: "I'm going to beat them all before I retire, to prove that I am the greatest of all time" (Hauser 350). The fight was on for February 15, 1978.

Unfortunately for Ali, interest in the bout waned. Most fans probably assumed that it would be no contest. When Lewis tried to get him to put on his usual prefight running of the mouth, the champion refused, saying that he would look stupid bad mouthing an obviously inferior fighter. Ali's overconfidence also led to minimal training. He sparred just a few dozen rounds as his weight ballooned to 242 pounds (which he did manage to lower before the weigh in).

The fight itself was a farce, at least from Ali's standpoint. He tried the rope-a-dope strategy for a few rounds, but Spinks simply did not tire as he pounded away at Ali's body. The champ never really mounted a serious attack until the final round when he managed to land solid blows with Leon against the ropes, but it was too late. In a split decision, the unthinkable had happened. Just as in 1964 when Cassius Clay a prohibitive underdog, beat Sonny Liston, Leon Spinks, won the heavyweight championship.

Ali was disconsolate after the fight, but in the ritual post-bout press conference he refused to grouse about the decision: "I messed up; I was lousy.... [Spinks] fought a good fight. He made fools of everybody, even me." Years later Ali admitted to Thomas Hauser, "Of all the fights I lost in boxing, losing to Spinks hurt the most" (Hauser 353). Once he was back in Chicago, Ali seemed almost on the verge of manic depression. Promoter Harold Smith, a guest in Ali's house the night after the fight, was amazed to see him run out of his front door at two in the morning, muttering, "Gotta' get my title back." He then took off for some road work. Smith drove behind him, deeply concerned, as Ali stopped his running to shadow box under a street light, all the time muttering, "Gotta' get my title back" (Hauser 355).

And he did. The rematch took place on September 15, 1978, at the New Orleans Super Dome. Almost 65,000 people packed the venue, in spite of the fact that the fight was being broadcast live on ABC. The $4,800,000 gate almost doubled the previous record, set in the 1927 Jack Dempsey–Gene Tunney fight, and the Ali–Spinks rematch drew the second largest TV audience in history, after the famed mini-series, *Roots*. Ali revised his strategy, avoiding the rope-a-dope, fighting in the middle of the ring, and always trying to close each round with a flurry of punches. It worked; Ali won a unanimous decision. In the words of Howard Cosell, "Objectively speaking it was a terrible fight." Nonetheless, when it became clear near the end that Ali was in control, thousands of fans urged him on. Millions of fans watched throughout the world. And Cosell caught the drama of the moment, when he closed his broadcast with some lyrics from singer Bob Dylan's "Forever Young," a profoundly felt compliment to his aging friend (Hauser 360).

Muhammad Ali achieved something most thought was impossible. He recaptured the heavyweight championship for a third time. After the second Spinks fight, he seemed to recognize that he was not, in fact, forever young. After the bout he told a reporter, "I'd be the biggest fool in the world to go out a loser after being the first three-time champ." Besides, he worried that other black athletes such as Joe Louis had stayed around too long. He didn't want to follow in their footsteps: "My people need one black man to come out on top" (Hauser 361). Nine months later, Ali confirmed this realization when he officially announced his retirement. He said that he had a lot to do. He wanted to be with his family. Besides, he was in a new TV miniseries, costarring with Kris Kristoferson. Also, President Jimmy Carter was interested in sending Ali to Africa on a goodwill mission with diplomatic overtones.[6] Carter even thought about posting him to Iran to help with the hostage crisis. It was time for the champion to step down.

And yet, a little more than a year later, Ali signed to fight Larry Holmes, a hard-hitting youngster and former Ali sparring partner, for the vacated World Championship, to be promoted by Don King. The Nevada Boxing Commission sanctioned the bout despite a Mayo Clinic report on Ali that showed possible brain damage and clear signs of a hyperthyroid condition. Ali had nothing to gain from the fight, except a lot of money from the gate, which surpassed the take at the second Spinks fight. Holmes battered him for 10 rounds before the referee stopped the slaughter. Afterwards, Holmes went to Ali's hotel room, apologized, and told him, "You're the greatest. I love you." Showing a bit of his old verbal spunk, Ali teasingly responded, "Man, now you got me mad.... And I'm coming back to whip your ass. Gimme Holmes" (Hauser 412).

Ali didn't get Holmes. Given problems with his kidney, his brain, and his thyroid, he shouldn't have gotten anyone. And yet he wanted one more shot at a victory. He signed to fight Trevor Berbick, who had lost to Holmes after his match with Ali, in Nassau in December 1981. As with the Holmes bout, Ali had nothing left. Berbick was the aggressor. Ali couldn't hit and he couldn't dance. It was a unanimous decision, more

Ali's loss than Berbick's victory. Now it really was time to retire, and Ali accepted the inevitable. As he told a press conference after the defeat: "Father Time caught up with me. I'm finished." But he couldn't help going out with a bit of that old braggadocio: "At least I didn't go down. No pictures of me on the floor,... no broken teeth, no blood. I'm happy I'm still pretty. I came out alright for an old man" (Hauser 430).[7] Muhammad Ali never appeared in a professional bout again.[8]

NOTES

1. Mobutu also encouraged King in his efforts to include a three-day black music festival as part of a total experience celebrating black culture. In a bizarre footnote, King had planned to unveil promotional banners featuring the slogan, "From Slave Ship to Championship." Zairian officials, sensitive about Africans' role in the slave trade, forced the promoter to burn them all (Cassidy 89).

2. The fight was scheduled to begin between 3:00 and 4:00 AM to take into account the time difference between Zaire and the United States and to accommodate theaters showing the bout on closed-circuit television, a fact of which the clever Ali was no doubt aware. His use of the image of the black ghetto also resonates with his attempts to place the U.S.-flag waving Foreman far removed from black street life.

3. Interestingly, many Africans apparently saw Ali as a hero well before the Foreman bout, and even before he converted to the Nation of Islam. According to historian Jonathan Zimmerman, a number of African American Peace Corps volunteers "proudly noted Africans' reverence for Cassius Clay, a symbol of Black power and defiance" in the early 1960s (Zimmerman 1023).

4. Interestingly, Ali and Norton became friends after they both retired. Norton was in a serious automobile accident and remembers little about the several weeks he spent in the hospital, except that Ali was one of the first people to visit him. "I remember looking up and there was this crazy man... doing magic tricks for me. He made a handkerchief disappear; he levitated.... Ali was there and his being there helped me" (Hauser 341).

5. Spinks fought a sixth bout before Ali agreed take him on—a draw against Scott LeDoux.

6. The mission did not go well. African heads of state, especially non-Muslim ones, did not appreciate receiving a mere athlete in a quasi-diplomatic role.

7. Why did Ali continue to fight, long after his prime? A number of his friends urged him not to. We've seen Ferdie Pacheco's pleas after the Shavers fight. After that same fight, Teddy Brenner, who ran Madison Square Garden, told Ali that he would never book him at the Garden again, so concerned was he about the champ's health. But Ali continued to fight. Part of the motivation was no doubt money. Ali continued to be extraordinarily generous to friends and strangers alike. For example, before the Shavers fight, he saw a bum in the streets

of New York and gave him a 100 dollar bill. Some of his hangers-on took advantage of him financially, while his manager, Herbert Muhammad, made some unwise financial decisions (as did Ali). As Ali said about the $8 million he was guaranteed for fighting Holmes, "Where else can I make that kind of money in an hour?" (Cassidy 137). But probably more than money, it was Ali's love of boxing and the glory of being a winner that spurred him on. As he wrote in *The Soul of a Butterfly*, "The truth is if I had won my last fight, I would have kept going. I would have been sixty years old still trying to achieve the impossible." Intellectually he knew that he risked physical damage by continuing to fight, but he concluded, "Whatever I suffered physically was worth what I have accomplished in my life" (Ali, *Butterfly* 131).

8. In an interesting footnote to Ali's boxing career, Joe Louis came to respect him. Louis believed he would have beaten the brash young champ had both met in their primes, but he also "recognized Ali's skills as a fighter" (Remnick 229). Ali learned to appreciate again the virtues of his childhood hero. In 1976, while training for a bout with Ken Norton, Ali invited Louis to his camp for 10 days and even offered him a gift of $30,000 to help the financially strapped ex-champ. Later, the two appeared on television together, after which Ali revealed to Louis that he had dreamed that he had knocked out Louis. Joe gave him a classic deadpan look and mock growled, "Don't you even dream it" (Mead 293). In late 1980, a few months before he died, Louis showed up in a wheelchair at an Ali press conference. Ali promised to copy the techniques that Louis had used against Max Schmeling in 1938 when Ali fought Larry Holmes. He also promised to visit Louis in his house. Louis died in April 1981 before Ali could pay that visit. And shortly after Louis's death, when reminded by a reporter that he had once called Louis an Uncle Tom, Ali reacted angrily: "I never said that, not that way, anyhow. That's demeaning. Look at Joe's life. Everybody loved Joe.... From black folks to redneck Mississippi crackers, [they] loved him. They're all crying. That shows you. Howard Hughes dies, with all his billions, not a tear. Joe Louis, everybody cried" (Remnick 229).

EPILOGUE:
THE REAL MUHAMMAD ALI

Muhammad Ali's retirement, like his career, has been marked with both lows and highs. His third marriage ended in divorce in 1986. A number of business ventures failed, including a well-meaning but undercapitalized plan to send powdered milk to third world countries and a wild scheme to raise a hundred billion dollars to build 300 mosques and 100,000 low-income housing units in America's 300 largest cities. Of most concern, however, was his health. In 1984, Ali was diagnosed with Parkinson's syndrome, a nonfatal neurological disorder, the result of years in the ring and a number of blows to the head. The main symptoms are diminished motor skills, slurred speech, and facial ticks. But these symptoms do not seem to have affected his mind.

On a more positive note, Ali has been married to his fourth wife, Lonnie, since 1986. She first met him as Cassius Clay when she was six years old and her family moved into a house across from his in Louisville. He has also been active in his religion, making numerous appearances at mosques around the country. In the 1980s and 1990s, he spent as many as 200 days a year on the road, making personal appearances. He even made an unofficial visit to Saddam Hussein in Iraq in 1990 in hopes of helping to defuse tensions between Iraq and the United States. Although war did come in January 1991, Ali helped secure the release of 15 U.S. hostages captured when Iraq invaded Kuwait. As Thomas Hauser noted in 1991, "Ali's good deeds are universally acknowledged" (Hauser 483).[1]

Perhaps the pinnacle of that acknowledgment occurred during the 1996 Summer Olympic Games in Atlanta. As a symbol of recognition, the International Olympic Committee (IOC) chose Ali to light the torch, officially opening the Games, in one of the most powerful moments in Olympic history. Atlanta resident and former Olympic gold medal winner Evander Holyfield carried the torch into the stadium to the delight and applause of the spectators. Holyfield and Greek runner Voula Patoulidou jointly carried it around the track, then passed the torch to U.S. swimmer and former gold medalist Janet Evans. She then mounted the steps toward the Olympic flame to the sound of Beethoven's "Ode to Joy" and the cheers of the crowd, who assumed that she would light the torch. Then, as she was part way up the steps, Ali emerged from the shadows, carried the torch to the top, and lit the flame. According to the Olympic Museum, "Tears flow[ed] easily and generously from the eyes of many spectators" ("Olympic Games: 1996 Atlanta Torch-Relay" 5).

In *The Soul of a Butterfly*, Ali says he remembers the lighting of the torch as "among the most memorable moments of my life." He is especially glad that the generation that had watched his career could be reintroduced to him and that "a whole new generation [would become] interested in [his] life story." He is proud that he could prove, even as his arm shook just a bit when he lit the flame, that Parkinson's syndrome "had not defeated" him. And still illustrating some of that old, familiar braggadocio, he concludes, "I showed them that I was still the greatest of all time." Poignantly, the Olympic Committee actually gave him the spent torch as a memento. In a moment reminiscent of his passion for that gold medal he won 36 years earlier, he took it back to his hotel room and stayed up all night, holding it in his hand. He says that the torch "hangs on a wall in my office, so I can see it every day" (Ali, *Butterfly* 181, 183).[2]

In a touching reprise of the ceremony, Ali also lit the torch for the 2002 Winter Games when it arrived in Atlanta from Greece in December 2001. He handed it to US figure skater Peggy Fleming, a gold medalist herself, to begin the first leg of the 13,500-mile trip to Salt Lake City. Georgia governor Roy Barnes said that "the Olympic Spirit overcomes fear, hate, and misunderstanding," a sentiment with which Muhammad Ali would surely agree ("Muhammad Ali Lights").

As of this writing, Ali lives in comfort with Lonnie in Berrien Springs, Michigan. He remains a faithful Muslim, still does personal appearances—as at the Indianapolis 500 in 2003—and is deeply involved in the foundation that bears his name, the Muhammad Ali Center for the Advancement of Humanity, which will open a new headquarters in downtown Louisville in November 2005. He has been increasingly recognized as a proponent of peace and reconciliation, receiving a United Nations Messenger of Peace Award in 1970. He even seemed only a little

worried when his daughter, Laila, began her boxing career in 1999 and
was cheered when he attended the bout in 2002 when she won her first
title. The Greatest is doing pretty well.

So how would he end a brief study of his life that focuses on his years
as a prizefighter? His recent memoir gives us a pretty good idea. His reflections on why he became a prizefighter have nothing to do with the part
of the American dream that trumpets the individual self and its economic and social mobility. It has everything to do with the kinder, gentler
side of that dream: to help others achieve a better, more free life. As he
writes in *Soul of a Butterfly*:

> When you saw me in the boxing ring fighting, it wasn't just so I
> could beat my opponent. My fighting had a purpose. I had to be
> successful in order to get people to listen to the things I had to say.
>
> I was fighting to win the world heavyweight title so I could go out
> in the streets and speak my mind. I wanted to go to the people,
> where unemployment, drugs, and poverty were part of everyday life.
> I wanted to be a champion who was accessible to everyone. I hoped
> to inspire others to take control of their lives and to live with pride
> and self-determination. I thought perhaps if they saw that I was
> living my life the way I chose to live it—without fear and with
> determination—they might dare to take the risk that could set them
> free.
>
> I knew that my boxing career wouldn't last long. I had to be loud,
> proud and confident. The world was watching and I knew that
> many people did not like everything about me. But sometimes all
> you have to do is breathe, and people will have an opinion on how
> you drew that breath. I couldn't live the way that others wanted me
> to live. If I had stayed in Louisville and never become a boxer, I
> could have died and it would never have made any news. But
> because I was boxing, and winning, when I said something people
> took notice. I had to use that attention to advance my real purpose.
> (Ali, *Butterfly* 69)[3]

And perhaps this is the real Muhammad Ali, masks discarded, standing
in the middle of life's ring. Those masks were in part designed for a
greater purpose. No doubt he had many personas. He could be angry,
petulant, selfish, unfaithful, profligate, and naïve. He could also be warm,
generous, loving, extraordinarily witty, with the instincts of a true showman, and above all true to his beliefs. He could be simultaneously a child
and a man. Muhammad Ali was also clearly one of the greatest athletes

of all time. But he also transcended his sport to become a powerful symbol for the United States in a time of profound domestic and foreign crises. He was a villain to some but ultimately became a hero to most. His reach spanned the globe. Muhammad Ali, warts and all, was, finally, truly the King of the World, a world in which everybody knew his name.

NOTES

1. Of course, not everyone sings Ali's praises. A veteran of the Vietnam War known simply as "Irish Jim" says, "I never could understand how someone whose profession it was to enter a roped off area with the intention of knocking the brains out of another human could be against the concept of war?" (Irish Jim, e-mail to the author, June 19, 2005), while another, Nicholas Andreacchio, notes simply, "At the time, I was not in sympathy with him and I am still not" (Nick Andreacchio, e-mail to the author, June 19, 2005).

2. In another act of reconciliation, the IOC also presented Ali with a gold medal to replace the one he had thrown into the Ohio River.

3. Significantly, in a recent poll generated on Ali's Web page, people were asked, "What does Muhammad Ali mean to you?" Over half responded "Personal Hero" (http://www.ali.com).

BIBLIOGRAPHY

"Ali." http://www.ali.com/vote.cfm?qid=4&result=1 (accessed June 19, 2005).

Ali, Muhammad, with Richard Durham. *The Greatest: My Own Story.* New York: Random House, 1975.

Ali, Muhammad, with Hana Yasmeen Ali. *The Soul of a Butterfly: Reflections of Life's Journey.* New York: Simon and Schuster, 2004.

Anderson, Dave. "I Didn't Dance, That Was the Trick." *New York Times,* October 31, 1974, 55.

Bingham, Howard, and Max Wallace. *Muhammad Ali's Greatest Fight: Cassius Clay vs. the United States of America.* New York: M. Evans and Company, 2000.

"Biography of Malcolm X." http://www.africawithin.com/malcolmx/malcolm_bio.htm (accessed October 4, 2004).

Brown, Claude. *Manchild in the Promised Land.* New York: Simon and Schuster, 1999.

Brunt, Stephen. *Facing Ali: The Opposition Weighs In.* Guilford, Conn.: The Lyons Press, 2002.

"Capricorn." http://www.astrology-online.com/capricrn.htm (accessed August 4, 2004).

Cassidy, Robert. *Muhammad Ali: The Greatest of All Time.* Chicago: Publishers International, 1999.

"Chinese Zodiac." http://www.chinatoday.com/culture/zodiac/zodiac.htm. Accessed 4 August 2004.

Cosell, Howard. *Cosell.* New York: Pocket Books, 1974.

Cottrell, John. *Muhammad Ali, Who Once Was Cassius Clay.* New York: Funk and Wagnalls, 1967.

Edmonds, A. O. *Joe Louis*. Grand Rapids: William B. Eerdmans, 1973.

Edwards, Harry. *The Revolt of the Black Athlete*. New York: Free Press, 1970.

Fleischer, Nat. *John L. Sullivan: Champion of Champions*. New York: G. P. Putnam's Sons, 1951.

Frazier, Joe, with Phil Berger. *Smokin' Joe: The Autobiography of a Heavyweight Champion of the World, Smokin' Joe Frazier*. New York: Macmillan, 1996.

Freedman, Suzanne. *Clay v. the United States: Muhammad Ali Objects to the War*. Springfield, N.J.: Enslow Publishers, 1997.

Gallup, Dr. George H. *The Gallup Poll: Public Opinion, 1935–1971, Volume Three, 1959–1971*. New York: Random House, 1972.

Gorn, Elliott, ed. *Muhammad Ali: The People's Champ*. Urbana: University of Illinois Press, 1995.

Hano, Arnold. *Muhammad Ali: The Champion*. New York: G. P. Putnam's Sons, 1977.

Hauser, Thomas. *Muhammad Ali: His Life and Times*. New York: Simon and Schuster, 1991.

Johnson, Alexander. *Ten and Out: The Complete Story of the Prize Ring in America*. New York: Washburn, 1945.

Kane, Martin. "Three for Some Guests." *Sports Illustrated*, September 19, 1960.

Keyes, Ralph. "Why We Misquote." http://www.ralphkeyes.com/pages/books/niceguys/excerpt.htm (accessed March 9, 2005).

King, Martin Luther, Jr. *Why We Can't Wait*. New York: Signet, 1964.

Kram, Mark. *Ghosts of Manila: The Fateful Blood Feud Between Muhammad Ali and Joe Frazier*. New York: Harper Collins, 2001.

Lardner, John. *White Hopes and Other Tigers*. Philadelphia: J.B. Lippincott, 1951.

Lipsyte, Robert. *Free to Be Muhammad Ali*. New York: Harper and Row, 1978.

Louis, Joe. *My Life Story*. New York: Duell, Sloan and Pearce, 1947.

Mailer, Norman. *The Fight*. Boston: Little, Brown and Company, 1975.

Marqusee, Mike. *Redemption Song: Muhammad Ali and the Spirit of the Sixties*. London: Verso, 1999.

McRae, Donald. *Heroes without a Country: America's Betrayal of Joe Louis and Jesse Owens*. New York: Harper Collins, 2002.

Mead, Chris. *Champion Joe Louis: Black Hero in White America*. New York: Viking, 1986.

"Muhammad Ali's Daughter to Make Pro Boxing Debut." http://www.cnn.com/US/9910/07/ali.daughter/ (accessed June 19, 2005).

"Muhammad Ali Lights Olympic Torch in Atlanta." http://www.rediff.com/sports/2001/dec/05flame.htm (accessed June 19, 2005).

Narayanan, Vivian. "Only Connect." *Villiage Voice Book Reviews*. http://www.villagevoice.com/books/0412,narayanan,52021,10.html (accessed June 19, 2005).

Nash, Roderick. *The Nervous Generation: American Thought, 1917–1930*. Chicago: Rand McNally, 1970.

Olsen, Jack. *Black Is Best: The Riddle of Cassius Clay*. New York: G. P. Putnam's Sons, 1967.

Olsen, Jack. *The Black Athlete: A Shameful Story*. New York: Time-Life Books, 1968.

"Olympic Games: 1996 Atlanta Torch-Relay." http://www.olympic-museum.de/torches/torch1996.htm (accessed June 19, 2005).

Pacheco, Ferdie. *Muhammad Ali: A View from the Corner*. New York: Carol Publishers, 1992.

Plimpton, George. *Shadow Box*. New York: G.P. Putnam's Sons, 1977.

Remnick, David. *King of the World*. New York: Vintage Books, 1998.

Riess, Steven A., ed. *Major Problems in American Sport History*. Boston: Houghton Mifflin, 1997.

Roberts, Randy. *Papa Jack: Jack Johnson and the Era of White Hopes*. New York: The Free Press, 1983.

Roberts, Randy, and James Olson. *Winning Is the Only Thing: Sports in America Since 1945*. Baltimore: Johns Hopkins University Press, 1989.

Sammons, Jeffrey. *Beyond the Ring: The Role of Boxing in American Society*. Champaign-Urbana: University of Illinois Press, 1990.

Tessitore, John. *Muhammad Ali: The World's Champion*. New York: Franklin Watts, 1998.

Torres, Jose, and Bert Randolph Sugar. *Sting Like a Bee: The Muhammad Ali Story*. New York: Curtis Books, 1971; reprint, Chicago: Contemporary Books, 2002.

Tunis, John. *The American Way in Sport*. New York: Duell, Sloan, and Pearce, 1958.

van Every, Edward. *Joe Louis: Man and Super Fighter*. New York: Frederick A. Stokes Company, 1936.

Wells, Tom. *The War Within: America's Battle over Vietnam*. Berkeley: University of California Press, 1994.

Woodward, Bob, and Scott Armstrong. *The Brethren: Inside the Supreme Court*. New York: Simon and Schuster, 1979.

Young, A. J., Jr. "Joe Louis, Symbol." PhD diss., University of Maryland, 1968.

Zimmerman, Jonathan. "Beyond Double Consciousness: Black Peace Corps Volunteers in Africa, 1961–1971." *Journal of American History* (December 1995): 999–1028.

INDEX

About the Author

ANTHONY O. EDMONDS is Professor of History at Ball State University in Muncie, Indiana. He is author of *The War in Vietnam* (Greenwood, 1998).